KV-028-122

O W H Longhurst.

KA 0299655 3

UNI
WINCHES

RIPON

Ronald P. Jones, Photo.]

RIPON CATHEDRAL FROM THE FOOTBRIDGE OVER THE SKELL.

THE CATHEDRAL CHURCH OF

RIPON

A SHORT HISTORY OF THE CHURCH & A DESCRIPTION OF ITS FABRIC

BY

CECIL HALLETT, B.A.

MAGDALEN COLL., OXFORD

 WITH 53  ILLUSTRATIONS

LONDON GEORGE BELL & SONS 1901

UNIVERSITY COLLEGE WINCHESTER
LIBRARY

UNIVERSITY COLLEGE
WINCHESTER

M 00089 60KA

726.6
18A2

02996553

PREFACE.

THE original authorities for the history (both constitutional and architectural) of the Church of Ripon have been most ably edited for the Surtees Society by the Rev. Canon J. T. Fowler, F.S.A., in his *Memorials of Ripon* and *The Ripon Chapter Acts* (*Surtees Soc.*, vols. 74, 78, 81, 64). These authorities range from the Saxon period to the times following the Reformation, but in the Introductions to vol. 81, and in the Rev. J. Ward's *Fasti Riponienses*, included in vol. 78, the story is virtually continued to our own day; while the aforesaid Introductions epitomise, in its constitutional and architectural aspects, the whole history of the church.

To these volumes and to their Editor, who most kindly consented to revise the proofs of this book, the present writer is very deeply indebted. He has also had recourse to an article by Sir G. Gilbert Scott, R.A., in vol. xxxi. of the *Archæological Journal*; to the same Author's *Recollections*; to several articles on the Saxon Crypt, duly specified on pp. 76, 77; to the Guides, by J. R. Walbran, F.S.A., published by Mr. Harrison of Ripon; to Mr. Murray's *Cathedrals*; to the volume by the Ven. Archdeacon Danks in Messrs. Isbister's Cathedral Series; to *A Day in the City of Ripon*, by Mr. George Parker of Ripon; to the old Guides by Farrer and Gent respectively; and to other works of a more general character.

His sincere thanks are also due to the Right Rev. the Bishop of Ripon for permission to consult the library at the Palace; to the Very Rev. the Dean for privileges granted in connection with the library in the Cathedral and with the Cathedral itself; to the Ven. the Archdeacon of Ripon and the Ven. the Archdeacon of Richmond for their courteous assistance on several occasions; to Mr. J. T. Micklethwaite, V.P.S.A., Mr. W. H. St. John Hope, Mrs. Swire, the Rev. H. A. Wilson, Fellow of Magdalen College, the Rev. G. W. Garrod, and Mr. John Whitham for valuable information on various points, historical and architectural; to Mr. Ronald P. Jones for his excellent photographs, to the Archæological Institute and other learned Societies for various other illustrations, and to the Rev. E. H. Swann, the Rev. J. Beanland, Capt. E. J. Warre Slade, R.N., Mr. F. Forbes Glennie, Mr. T. Wall, Mr. Watson, and others for similar assistance.

He desires also to express his thanks to Mr. E. W. Winser, Dean's Verger, for much valuable local information; to Mr. Henry Williams, Canons' Verger, for expert advice on points of masonry; and to both, as well as to the Sexton, for that general assistance which they so willingly rendered him throughout his investigation of the Fabric.

CONTENTS.

LIST OF ILLUSTRATIONS.

A

Ronald P. Jones, Photo.]

THE NAVE—SOUTH SIDE.

(Showing junction of Transitional and Perpendicular work in the Tower.

Ronald P. Jones, Photo.]

VIEW FROM THE SOUTH-WEST.

RIPON CATHEDRAL.

CHAPTER I.

HISTORY OF THE CHURCH.

THERE is evidence that the neighbourhood of Ripon was inhabited during, and perhaps before, the Roman occupation of Britain. Whether the place was a settlement of the Romans is uncertain; but it was assuredly in touch with their civilization, for several of their roads passed near it—notably Watling Street, on which, six miles to the east, was Isurium, the modern Aldborough; while imperial coins and other Roman objects have been dug up in Ripon itself. It is not known whether the Romans imparted to the local tribes of the Brigantes their own Christianity; but two centuries after the withdrawal of the legions the greater part of what is now Yorkshire was absorbed by the invading Angles into their kingdom of Deira, which had itself been united with the more northern kingdom of Bernicia to form the single realm of Northumbria. Deira, however, seems to have retained its own individuality. About the year 627 King Eadwine of Northumbria was converted to Christianity by Paulinus, and the majority of his Deiran subjects followed his example.

The Scottish Monastery.—It is in the middle of the seventh century that the recorded history of Ripon begins. Deira was then ruled by Prince Alchfrith of Northumbria under his father, King Oswiu, nephew of Eadwine, and Bede, writing not eighty years after the event, relates that the prince chose Ripon for the site of a monastery. The date may be fixed in or just before the year 657. This monastery was one of those numerous religious colonies which were the result not only of the new Christian fervour, but also of a reaction from war toward social life and industry. It did not represent the Roman Christianity of Augustine which Paulinus had introduced into Deira from Canterbury, but the Christianity which had come from Ireland through St. Columba's missionary college at Iona, and which was now predominant throughout the north. The monks of Ripon were brought from Melrose Abbey on the Tweed. Like most monks of that early period, they probably followed no definite Rule. Their abbot was Eata, a pupil of St. Aidan, and previously Abbot of Melrose and Lindisfarne, while the guest-master was no less a person than Cuthbert, the legend of whose having entertained an angel unawares at Ripon added, no doubt, to the growing reputation of the house.

Its tranquillity, however, was not to last. The Roman party in the Northumbrian Church, though inconsiderable, was gaining force, and Alchfrith, deserting his former convictions, gave the new monastery, with an endowment of thirty or forty hides of land, as Bede relates, to one who had visited Rome, and who regarded the Irish (or, as it was called by that time, the Scottish) Church as schismatical.

The life of **St. Wilfrid of Ripon**—so full of adventure, misfortune, and lasting achievement—can only be related here in so far as it bears upon the story of this, his favourite monastery. It was in 661 that the transference from Eata to Wilfrid took place, and at once the Scottish monks, refusing to conform to Roman usages, left Ripon in a body. It is probable that Wilfrid imposed upon their successors the Benedictine Rule, which he had studied at Rome. The new Abbot was not yet in priest's orders, but was presently ordained at Ripon by Agilbert, the Frankish Bishop of Wessex. In 664 he took the action for which he is especially remembered in English history. Appearing at the Synod of Whitby, he prevailed upon King Oswiu to throw in his lot with the Roman party, and was thus the means indirectly of preventing the isolation of the England of that time from the Church and civilization of the Continent. Almost immediately afterwards Abbot Wilfrid became Bishop of Northumbria, and this tenure of the two offices by the same person was perhaps the origin of the subsequent connection of Ripon with the Archbishops of York.[1] Wilfrid insisted on going to be consecrated by Agilbert, who was now Bishop of Paris, and so long did he remain abroad that on his return in 666 he found another bishop, Chad (afterwards St. Chad of Lichfield), in possession of the see. He therefore retired to Ripon for three years, during which, however, he visited Mercia and also Kent, where he met Aedde, or Eddius, who became his chaplain and biographer.

The Saxon Monastery.—In 669 Wilfrid was restored to his see by Theodore, Archbishop of Canterbury, and soon afterwards began to build at Ripon. The Scottish monastery, which was probably of wood, is thought to have occupied a site between Priest Lane, Stonebridgegate,[2] and a nameless road which connects them. Wilfrid now abandoned it, and erected upon a new site a more imposing monastery of stone.[3] The practice of building in stone seems to have become uncommon in Britain after the departure of the Romans, and Wilfrid is thought to have employed foreign

[1] The archbishopric of York arose out of the bishopric of Northumbria in the eighth century.

[2] The name in this form is modern. In common speech the street is always 'Stammergate,' which is probably a corruption of 'Stanbriggate.' The latter is the original name of the street, and appears frequently in mediæval records. It has reference to a stone bridge over a brook where the gas-works now are. The continuation of this street toward the Cathedral is called St. Mary-gate, but this name again seems to be modern, and to have arisen from a notion that 'St. Mary-gate' is the origin of the word 'Stammergate'—a notion which would be rendered more plausible by the fact that this was the situation of the Lady-kirk.

[3] The question whether his monastery church stood over the Saxon crypt which exists below the present Cathedral is reserved for Chap. III.

workmen, perhaps Italians.[1]   His church is described by
Eddius, himself now a Ripon monk, as "of smoothed stone
from base to summit, and supported on various columns and
(?) arcades (*porticibus*)," and was doubtless of that Italian type
which had become identified in Britain with the Roman party in
the Church, as opposed to the Scottish mission.   The Scottish
type of church consisted of a small aisle-less nave and square
chancel : the Italian type generally had aisles, and the altar
was usually raised upon a platform, beneath which was a crypt
called *confessio*.   A little later than 670 A.D. Wilfrid's new
minster was solemnly dedicated by him in honour of St. Peter,
in the presence of a great concourse of clergy and nobles,
headed by the King of Northumbria, Ecgfrith, the successor of
Oswiu.   The endowments seem to have included at this time
certain lands round Ripon which had belonged to the British
Church before the coming of the Angles, and to have been now
increased by grants—some as far distant as Lancashire—made
by the great men present at the ceremony.   Wilfrid himself
gave a splendid copy of the Gospels, written in gold upon
purple vellum, the beginning perhaps of a library.[2]   The
feasting was kept up for three days—indeed, no monastery
could have had for its church a more striking dedication.   And
for the next seven years Ripon must have shared the importance of the Abbot-Bishop, whose state rivalled that of the
king.   By persuading the queen to become a nun, however,
he presently lost the royal favour ; while the great size of the
diocese, which extended at last from the Forth to the Wash,
prevented the achievement of complete success in his episcopal
work.

As yet the see of Canterbury was the sole archbishopric,
and in 678 Archbishop Theodore —already known as an
organizer of the episcopate—was invited to the court of Northumbria.   With Ecgfrith's approval, but without consulting
Wilfrid, he divided the diocese into the three sees of Hexham,
York, and Lindsey, answering respectively to the tribal divisions
Bernicia, Deira, and the land of the Lindiswaras (Lincoln-

---

[1] For the place of Ripon in the theory of the direct connection of Saxon
architecture with the Comacine Guild of Italy, see *The Cathedral
Builders*, by Leader Scott, p. 139 *sqq.*
[2] An MS. which has been thought to be identical with Wilfrid's gift came
into the market recently, and has passed to America.

shire). Wise though this action was, it was naturally resented by Wilfrid, who appealed to the Pope—the first appeal of the kind ever made by an Englishman—and set out himself for Rome. He was destined not to return till 680, and even then to be kept out of his bishopric till 686. Ripon was now in the new diocese of York, but in 681 Theodore constituted yet another diocese, of which he made Ripon the cathedral town.

Of **Eadhead, First Bishop of Ripon** (681–686), little is known. Originally a priest at the court of Oswiu, he had accompanied the intruded bishop, Chad, when the latter sought consecration at Canterbury during Wilfrid's absence for consecration in Gaul. Eadhead had afterwards been appointed by Theodore to the see of Lindsey, and was translated thence to Ripon when Lindsey was recovered by the Mercians.

His tenure of his new office lasted for five years only, for in 686 Aldfrith, the successor of Ecgfrith, restored Wilfrid—not indeed to his original bishopric of Northumbria, but to a see which combined the lately-formed dioceses of Ripon and York.[1] Eadhead accordingly retired, and there were no more Bishops of Ripon for twelve centuries.

To Wilfrid was restored not only his bishopric, but also his monastery of Ripon, which he retained in peace for the next five years. At the end of that time a long dispute arose with Aldfrith, who was veering back to the diocesan partition of Theodore, and Wilfrid, deprived of his see for the third time, crossed over into Mercia. In 703 a synod was held at Austerfield, the King and Berhtwald, Archbishop of Canterbury, being present, when Wilfrid was actually asked to promise that he would cease to act as bishop, that he would accept the partition of Theodore, and that he would retire to Ripon and not leave the monastery without the king's permission.

Though he was now a man of seventy, he set out once more for Rome, and this time as before the Pope decided in his favour. Returning to Ripon in 705, he attempted to conciliate Aldfrith's successor Eadwulf, but in vain. In the same

---

[1] The Saint's return after his long exile is still commemorated at Ripon, early in August, on the first Saturday after Lammas Day, when a man dressed as a Saxon bishop and riding a grey horse is escorted through the streets.

year, however, Eadwulf was succeeded by Osred, and presently
another synod was held, this time at Nidd, seven miles south
of Ripon, when it was decided, in the presence of Osred and
the now relenting Berhtwald, that Wilfrid should have the
monastery and see of Hexham (resigning York) and the
monastery of Ripon, thus restored to him for the second
time.

In 709 he received a call to Mercia, which had already
twice received him in his adversity, and in which he had
accepted the bishopric of Leicester.   Immediately before his
departure he was at Ripon, where he kept his treasure, and
having a presentiment that he would never return, he bequeathed
a portion of his wealth to the monastery, appointed Tatberht
to succeed him as Abbot, and took an affecting farewell of the
whole community.   Arriving at his monastery of Oundle, in
Northamptonshire, he was seized with illness, and died there
on October 12 in the seventy-sixth year of his age.   The
body was placed on a car and carried in solemn procession to
Ripon, where it was buried on the south side of the high altar
in his own minster.

In 710 the anniversary of his death was kept at Ripon
with great solemnity, and out of such commemorations,
probably, arose the feast of his *Depositio*,[1] which was afterwards kept on every 12th of October.   According to Eddius
a remarkable phenomenon occurred on this occasion.   In
the evening the monastery was suddenly encircled with
brilliant light, as of day, and whether this was a display of
Northern Lights or not, it was regarded as a Divine testimony
to the sanctity of Wilfrid.   The story shows, at any rate, that
he was already beginning to be regarded as a saint, and it was
probably about this time that his name was coupled with St.
Peter's in the dedication of the Church.   Miracles were worked
at his tomb, and it became an object of pilgrimage ; but little
is known of the period immediately succeeding his death,
save that the dwellers around Ripon (as a twelfth century
writer, Eadmer, represents) first encouraged the cult of the
saint, then became disgusted at the crowds it drew, and finally
endeavoured to check it altogether.   Wilfrid was succeeded in
the abbacy by Tatberht, and history has recorded the names of

---

[1] This liturgical term sometimes refers to the *burial* of a saint, sometimes, as here, to the *death*.

three more abbots who followed each other toward the end of the eighth century, Botwine, Alberht, Sigred ; and of one of uncertain date, Uilden or Wildeng.[1] In 791 a noble named Eardwulf, who had plotted against Ethelred, then King of Northumbria, was put to death (as it was thought) at the monastery gate by the king's orders. The monks carried him 'with Gregorian chantings' to the precincts of the church, where they laid him out, but after midnight he was found within the building—a recovery which was regarded as miraculous.

Ripon did not escape the violence of the Danes. It is thought that about the year 860 they burned the town and did some damage to the church, and the remarkable mound known as **Ailcy Hill**,[2] near the Canons' Residence, and due east of the Cathedral, is probably a relic of some battle of this period. In the street-names too, all ending in 'gate' (which in the sense of 'way' is a Danish word), another trace may perhaps be found of their presence, as well as of the existence of a town at this early period. The town probably grew up around the monastery. It has been believed that a civic charter was granted by King Alfred in 886 ; but this is impossible, even if such charters were ever granted at this time, for Alfred had resigned all this part of England (which since about 839 had owned the overlordship of Wessex) to the Danes in 878.

One of the great events in Ripon history is the visit of Alfred's grandson **King Athelstan**. Yorkshire had lately been a separate Danish kingdom, but it passed under the direct rule of Wessex in 926, and it was either in that year that Athelstan came, or in 937, when he defeated the Scots and other northern rebels at Brunanburh. It was to this king that the church afterwards referred the grant of its most important privileges. Among these was that of **sanctuary**, by which homicides, thieves, debtors, etc., could flee to Ripon and live there under the protection of St. Wilfrid for a specified time. The area within which they were protected extended one mile from the church in every direction, and the limit was marked by eight crosses, the base of one of which is still to be seen on

---

[1] There is also mention of an Abbot Tylberht, but he may be the same as Tatberht.

[2] *I.e.*, 'Elves-how '—' the hill of fairies.' Coins of Aella and other early kings have been found in the hill.

the Sharow Road. The penalties for molesting refugees were afterwards graduated as follows:—between the limit and the graveyard wall, £18; within the graveyard, £36; within the choir (where the pursued sought the last possible refuge at the 'grythstool,' or chair of sanctuary), confiscation of goods and possible death. Those who took sanctuary were called 'gyrthmen' or 'grythmen' (from the Anglo-Saxon 'gryth' 'peace'), and undertook, among other things, to carry the banners before the relics of St. Wilfrid in certain processions. They were under the spiritual charge of a 'gryth-priest.' The protection of the outer sanctuary can hardly have been extended to Ripon men, as theoretically the whole town could then have committed crimes with impunity, and practically the criminals would not have been safe from their fellow-townsmen. Ripon debtors did indeed enjoy protection here at Rogation-tide, but as a rule men of Ripon would seek sanctuary at Durham or Beverley. Athelstan is also said to have granted to the church a jurisdiction over its lands independent alike of the northern archbishop and of the king, with the right to inflict the ordeals of fire and water, and with exemption from taking oaths, from taxation, and from military service.[1] Of the two charters in which these grants are set forth, one is indeed of the eleventh or twelfth, and the other of the thirteenth century, but Athelstan may at any rate have done something to give rise to the tradition, though it is impossible to tell exactly what. The story of his having given the manor to the see of York is doubtless misleading. The territorial sway of the Archbishop at Ripon must be of earlier origin, and it may even have arisen out of the grant of the monastery with its thirty or forty hides of land to Wilfrid and his retention of them after his elevation to the see of Northumbria.

The connection of the monastery with the Archbishop is illustrated in the reign of Athelstan's brother Eadred, when Archbishop Wulfstan, by aiding a rebellion for the purpose of again setting up a Danish king at York, drew down the royal anger upon Ripon. In 948 (or 950, according to one authority) Eadred harried Northumbria, and then, says the Worcester

---

[1] At a later period the Chapter claimed also that 'St Wilfrid's men' need not pay tolls when travelling on business through the realm, and on one occasion they issued to a Ripon clerk a kind of passport.

Chronicle, "was that famed minster burned at Ripon, which St. Wilfrid built." Wulfstan himself was deprived and imprisoned.

About two years later the half-ruined and deserted church was visited (the see of York being vacant) by Oda, Archbishop of Canterbury. There was a tradition in the sixteenth century that he rebuilt it, but his visit is also memorable for another tradition, namely, that he translated the bones of St. Wilfrid to Canterbury. Hence arose a fierce dispute between Canterbury and Ripon, each claiming that it possessed the body of the Saint. The claim of Canterbury, which is accepted to this day by the Church of Rome, is supported by the assertion of Oda himself, and by several subsequent chroniclers, one of whom, however, attributes the translation to St. Dunstan, while another goes so far as to concede that Oda left a portion of the bones behind. But Ripon always maintained that it possessed the whole, and that the relics removed had been those of Wilfrid II. (Archbishop of York, 718–732). According to the contemporary biographer of Oswald (Archbishop of York, 972–992) the bones of the Saint were at Ripon in the tenth century, and Oswald solemnly enshrined them— whence that feast of St. Wilfrid's translation which was afterwards kept on the 24th of April ; and a later chronicler speaks of "the body of the blessed Wilfrid" as being at Ripon in the reign of Stephen. The claim of Canterbury was forgotten for a time in the glories of St. Thomas à Becket, while that of Ripon became more or less established in the north. In 1224 Archbishop de Gray, who translated the alleged relics at Ripon to a more splendid shrine, declared that he had found the skeleton complete. In the fifteenth century Henry V. himself writes to Ripon of his reverence for "St. Wilfrid, buried in the said church." In the sixteenth, Leland, while recording a common opinion that Oda rebuilt the minster, makes no mention of any removal of the relics. The controversy will perhaps never be decided definitely, but it is interesting in view of the cult of St. Wilfrid at Ripon in the middle ages.

The account of the enshrinement of the relics by Oswald has been thought to imply that it was he who rebuilt the monastery, and that he filled it again with monks. Whether it was rebuilt by Oda or Oswald, the body of St. Cuthbert rested here in 995 on its way from Chester-le-Street to Durham. From this point onwards, however, no more is heard of monks at Ripon, and it may be interesting to recall here the part which this monastery had played in the history of the Church. Its first abbot, Eata, had become Bishop of Hexham and of Lindisfarne. It had been for a time the home of St. Cuthbert. Under Wilfrid, Ceolfrith, one of its monks, had become Abbot of Wearmouth, and another, Æthelwald, had carried on Cuthbert's work in the Farne Islands. In accepting and treasuring the staff of St. Columba, the Ripon of Wilfrid had forgotten something of its hostility to the Scottish mission. Through Wilfrid, Ripon had been connected with the founding of other monasteries, Hexham, Selsey, Lichfield, Oundle. Through his labours, again, and those of St. Willibrord, another of its monks, it had become known as a great centre of missionary work. Wilfrid had strengthened Christianity in Mercia and Kent, and may claim to have introduced it into Sussex and the Isle of Wight. Abroad he had carried the Gospel to the Frisians, and his work among them was splendidly completed by Willibrord, who became Archbishop of Utrecht.[1]

The College of Secular Canons.—From 995 to the Conquest, the history of Ripon is almost a blank. During that time the monastery, by a reversal of the more usual process, became converted into a college of secular canons, but nothing is known of the manner in which the change was effected. The last Saxon Archbishop of York, Ealdred, who crowned both Harold and the Conqueror, is said to have founded prebends—perhaps giving lands out of his manor, and the Canons of Ripon duly appear in Domesday Book (1085-6). In 1070 the Conqueror, to whom the north had given much difficulty, ordered the Vale of York to be harried. Ripon suffered severely, and in Domesday Book the surrounding lands are recorded as "waste." The minster probably shared in the general wreck.

What happened to it in the succeeding period is not definitely known. It may have been entirely rebuilt, as most great Saxon churches were after the Conquest, or it may have been rebuilt partially, or merely enlarged. That

---

[1] Frisia's debt was remembered in the seventeenth century, when one of the Canons of Antwerp wrote an account of Ripon monastery for his countrymen.

something was done is proved by the existence south of the
choir of some Norman work which has been attributed to the

Rev. J. Beanland, Photo.]

EARLY APSIDAL CHAPEL WITH LATER CHAPEL SUPERIMPOSED.

first Norman Archbishop, Thomas of Bayeux (1070–1100),
or to Archbishop Thurstan (1114–1141).

The former died at Ripon. Indeed, the Archbishops had been in the habit of residing here since the end of the tenth century, and they duly appear in Domesday Book as lords of the manor, of which the canons' land is apparently treated as a part. It is worthy of note that Domesday Book records also the 'soc' jurisdiction and freedom from taxation which are mentioned in the 'Athelstan' charters. The exemption also from the king's officers which is set forth in the same charters, was proved in 1106, when an attempted invasion of the liberties of the Church by the Sheriff of York was successfully resisted by Archbishop Gerard before arbitrators appointed by Henry I. This king also exempted the lands of Ripon from castle-building, and granted to the Canons and the Archbishop a fair at the feast of St. Wilfrid's translation (April 24th). In the next century fairs were also claimed for the feast of his *Depositio* (October 12th), and for the feasts of St. Michael and of the Finding of the Holy Cross.

Archbishop Thomas II. (1109–1114) founded the **Hospital of St. John the Baptist,** and another Hospital, that **of St. Mary Magdalen,** of which the chapel remains, was founded by his successor, **Archbishop Thurstan** (1114–1141). Both these Hospitals were affiliated to the Church, and the masterships were in the gift of the Archbishop. St. John's afforded shelter to poor travellers who came in through the forest which then adjoined the town. When the forest was cleared, the endowment provided exhibitions for a few poor boys, who lived here while they pursued their studies in "grammar" (perhaps at the Grammar School), with a view to becoming clerks. The two hospitals, and a third which was founded later, were placed at three of the principal entrances to the town, with the express intention, perhaps, of assisting the pilgrims who resorted to the shrine of St. Wilfrid.

Thurstan added one more canon to the staff by founding the prebend of Sharow. He may also be called the founder of Fountains Abbey, which was built on land assigned by him out of his domain of Ripon.

In the troubles of the reign of Stephen, Ripon took no small share. When the Scots descended into Yorkshire, nominally to aid the Empress Maud, Thurstan sent against them all the levies which an archbishop, as a feudal baron, could muster, including doubtless the men of his manor of Ripon, and the victory which they won near Northallerton in 1138 is known as the Battle of the Standard, from the banners of the three mother-churches—Ripon, York, and Beverley—which waved over the English army. Ripon was soon to experience the anarchy which prevailed toward the end of the war. In 1140 Alan, Earl of Richmond, entrenched himself on a neighbouring hill and grievously oppressed the town and its inhabitants. Led by him, the large landholders in the neighbourhood broke open the storehouses and granaries of the archbishop, and in 1143 Earl Alan himself burst into the church with an armed band and attacked Archbishop William Fitzherbert (afterwards St. William of York), who was standing by St. Wilfrid's shrine. The Archbishop's offence may have been that he was the king's nephew. At any rate he was detested by the Cistercians, who were strongly represented here by Fountains Abbey, and Ripon seems to have sided with them, for in 1148, when Archbishop William was temporarily deprived of his office, it was to Ripon that his supplanter, Archbishop Murdac, retired when he durst not enter York. Stephen confirmed to the College all the privileges granted by his predecessors.

Building of the Present Church.—The reign of Henry II. is marked by another rebuilding of the church. William was succeeded in 1154 (the year of the king's accession) by **Archbishop Roger de Pont l'Evêque** (1154-1181). This prelate is known in politics for his opposition to Thomas à Becket, and in art for his prominent share in the development of our national architecture. There is perhaps no more important example of the transition from the Norman to the Early English style than his work at Ripon. With the exception of the crypt under the present crossing, and of some Norman work south of the present choir, he rebuilt the whole church, and history has recorded the wording of a deed in which he gives " £1000 of the old coinage for the building of, the basilica . . . which we have begun afresh." [1] Roger's church was a cruciform building, and its nave had no aisles. A great portion of his work remains—the two transepts, half of the central tower, and

---

[1] Until Walbran drew attention to this passage, the rebuilding was attributed to Thurstan.

portions of the nave and choir.   The plan (see below, p. 67) was
typical of the early history of the place and of its subsequent con-
version from a monastery into a college of secular canons; for
the aisleless cruciform arrangement in churches was developed
from a combination of the Scottish type with the Roman or
basilican, and the absence of aisles was, or rather had been
at a slightly earlier period, the recognized mark of a secular
as opposed to a monastic church.   In giving aisles to the
choir Roger's plan was singular, for it was not usual for a
choir to have aisles when the nave had none.   Except by
the addition of nave-aisles, the dimensions of his plan (as
Walbran remarked) have not been materially exceeded; and
Ripon is an example of the size to which churches of canons
often attained, in spite of the fact that their plan was generally
that of a mere parish church.

The next archbishop, Geoffrey Plantagenet, was often in
disagreement with his brothers, Richard I. and John, but the
manor of Ripon is said to have been the only portion of his
temporalities of which the latter king did not deprive him.

After Geoffrey's death the see was vacant for nine years until
1216, the year of the accession of Henry III., when it was
given to **Archbishop Walter de Gray** (1216-1255).   In
the same year 'spiritual fraternity' was formally concluded
between Ripon and Fountains; and a somewhat similar
arrangement was made a little later with Southwell,
which since Henry I. had shared with Ripon and Beverley
the dignity of a mother-church or pro-cathedral in the diocese
of York.   In 1224, at the request of the Canons, Archbishop
de Gray translated the relics of St. Wilfrid (if such they were)
to a new shrine, enshrining the head separately in such a way
that it was exposed to view.   He also granted an indulgence of
thirty days to all who should make pilgrimage to the saint's
new resting-place.   This second translation never became a
feast, but it doubtless stimulated the cult of St. Wilfrid afresh,
and probably brought considerable profit to the Church.

A few years later, at any rate, an important alteration was
made in the fabric, by the building of the present west front
with its two flanking towers, and the tall wooden and lead-
covered spires which once crowned the latter and the central
tower were probably erected at this period.

In 1230, the Archbishop founded a seventh prebend—

that of Stanwick ; and in 1241 sanctioned the addition of the parish of Nidd to the common property of the College.

Watson, Ripon, Photo.]

THE WEST FRONT BEFORE SIR G. G. SCOTT'S RESTORATION.

(From an old print, by the kind permission of the Ripon Museum.)

As yet, most of the prebends were distinguished by the names of the Canons who held them, or of Saints ; and it

B

was not till 1301 that they were named after the principal hamlet or township in each—Stanwick, Monkton, Givendale, Sharow, Nunwick, Studley, Thorp. They were all in the neighbourhood except Stanwick, which was in the North Riding, near Richmond. The Church was (as it still is) parochial as well as collegiate. Each prebend carried with it a cure of souls, yet all (except Stanwick) were included in the huge parish of Ripon, which extended to Pateley Bridge, and in 1300 had a radius of nine or ten miles. Thus the collegiate establishment differed from the usual type in which each prebend was a separate parish with a church of its own. Moreover, there was neither Dean nor Chancellor. The Canons may at first have lived in common, but as early as 1301, and probably earlier, they were dwelling in separate prebendal houses round the Church. There is no evidence that they ever resided on their prebends, except in the case of the Canon of Sharow, whose residence was at that place. The canonries, having been founded by Archbishops of York, were in the gift of the see, or of the Crown when the see was vacant. The Canon of Stanwick was *ex officio* Ruler of the Choir, whence his obligation to reside in Ripon in spite of the remoteness of his prebend, which was served by a vicar. Similarly the Canon of Monkton was always Treasurer, and had charge of the Chapter-house, the ornaments and plate, and the High Altar.

The revenues of the church may be divided as usual under three heads. There was a Common Fund, arising from certain rents, tithes, fees, and oblations ; a survival perhaps of a time when the Canons lived in common. Secondly, there were the revenues drawn by the Canons from their respective prebends, and consisting partly of rents, but chiefly of tithes. The prebend of Stanwick was worth about twice as much as any other. Thirdly, there was the Fabric Fund, arising from certain rents, oblations,[1] and licences, from the profits of St. Wilfrid's burning-iron (with which cattle were branded to keep off murrain),[2] and, in later days, of the pok-stone (which was probably regarded as in some way a preventive against the 'pokkes' of sheep and cattle) ; but especially from the farm

---

[1] Especially at St. Wilfrid's shrine.

[2] It has been suggested that this was the iron which in Saxon times had been used for the ordeal of fire.

of indulgences. When much building was in progress the Canons' incomes were afterwards specially taxed, and once or twice Peter's-pence were actually withheld from the Pope and devoted to architectural purposes.

At the time of Archbishop de Gray, the old and somewhat vague jurisdictions in and about Ripon had become more distinct. The parish was a Peculiar,[1] and as such was exempt from the authority of the Archdeacon of Richmond, either by tradition from the days when the church was a monastery, or because of the presence here of the Arch-bishops. Over this Peculiar (the laity included) the Chapter exercised the spiritual jurisdiction of an archdeacon's court, assisted by the Rural Dean of Ripon, who sat as 'Dean of Christianity.' This 'Court Christian' dealt with testament-ary and matrimonial cases, cases of defamation, immorality, neglect of religious duties, etc. Accused persons cleared themselves by compurgation, or underwent penalties (com-mutable, however), such as being beaten, walking barefoot in the processions, suspension *ab ingressu ecclesiæ*, or excom-munication.[2] Lesser offences were dealt with by an arch-bishop's officer called *penitentiarius*, who heard confessions and enjoined penances. The Archbishop was Ordinary of the Peculiar. He held visitations in the Chapter-house, and could order repairs of buildings, make statutes (in consultation with the Chapter) for the College, and sequestrate its revenues. He also exercised authority over offending Canons and over the in-ferior clergy of the staff, though the correction of these belonged primarily to the Chapter and especially to the Canon of Stanwick.

For purposes of secular jurisdiction Ripon, with the lands round it, was a Liberty, exempt, that is, from the authority of the Sheriff. The Liberty was almost co-extensive with the Peculiar. Within it were two secular jurisdictions, that of the Archbishop as lord of the manor, and that of the Chapter, which embraced the southern half of the town and many country districts, and which may have originated either with

---

[1] A Peculiar is a district taken out of its geographical surroundings for purposes of ecclesiastical jurisdiction (*Sir W. Anson*).

[2] In later times (at any rate) the Archbishop apparently had a spiritual court of his own. A Chapter minute of 1467 declares a certain person accused of a spiritual offence to be "non de foro Capituli sed de foro Archiepiscopi, unde litteræ correctionis emanârunt."

MEDIÆVAL SEALS.

1. Seal of the Mediæval Chapter.
2. Capitular Seal "ad causas."
3. Common Seal of the Vicars.

Ealdred's presumable gifts of land out of the manor to form prebends, or (as the charters pretend) from a grant of Athelstan, or perhaps from an original independence enjoyed by the church as a monastery. The Chapter claimed within their sphere the rights attributed to Athelstan's grant, and also assize of bread, ale, weights and measures ; dues of fairs and markets ; certain feudal dues ; power over masterless goods, and to deal with cases of rent, wrongful detention of land, and theft ; *cognitio de falso judicio;* execution of royal writs ; ' sheriff-tourn ' ; coroners of their own ; in fact the powers of a sheriff and of the justices-in-eyre, with a prison and the right of gaol-delivery, and even of inflicting capital punishment. In cases of homicide, however, a king's justice must sit as assessor. For civil suits there was a provision against ' wager of battle,' and the accused again cleared themselves by compurgation. Archbishop de Gray claimed similar privileges, but wished to exercise them over the whole Liberty, on the ground that the church and its appurtenances were part of his manor (as indeed they very possibly were, originally). Unlike Archbishop Gerard, who had supported the church's privilege against the sheriff, de Gray actually joined the sheriff in invading it. In 1228 the case came before the king's justices in the Chapter-house at Ripon, and the decision was for the Chapter. Thus the division of jurisdictions received from the State an undoubted sanction. Within his sphere the Archbishop appointed his own justices, but on arriving at the limits of that sphere, the king's justices sat with them there on the first day, and were afterwards admitted to sit with them in the town. The Archbishops claimed also that their commissioners should administer the oath of obedience at the mile-limit to those who sought sanctuary. The Archbishops are also said to have had a ' military court,' probably a feudal institution.

The memory of de Gray was perhaps held in scant respect at Ripon. He is accused by Matthew Paris of having refused to distribute his corn during a famine, and it was through the erection of Bishopthorpe Palace by him that Ripon ceased to be a favourite provincial residence of the Archbishops. Nevertheless they still frequently visited the town, both for sport and duty. They had a park " six miles in compass," and the fishing in the Ure. The existence, moreover, of a prison here for criminous clerks made the minster a convenient place for the public degradations which the Archbishop was obliged to hold from time to time. On these occasions the offending clerks were brought across to the church, where the Archbishop in full pontificals would hear their avowal of guilt in the nave, and then solemnly divest them of their robes and of their office at the west door.

In 1270 came the first echo from the outside world since the reign of Stephen. Prince Edward was setting out on a crusade, and Archbishop Giffard was compelled to exact from the Chapter a twentieth of their temporalities. The town had now attained to some importance, and sent two members to the Model Parliament of 1295.

As yet the minster of Archbishop Roger had suffered no change in its main fabric save the rebuilding of the west front, but an alteration was now to be made at the other extremity also, and the eastern portion of the choir was rebuilt with all the elaboration of the Decorated style. Of this work the greater part was probably effected under **Archbishop John Romanus** (1286–1296).

In 1293 the almost cathedral rank of the church was marked by the consecration within its walls of a bishop (of Galloway). It was, as has been said, the parish church of the huge parish of Ripon. Yet the town itself possessed at an early period a separate parish church of Allhallows, a memory of which survives in 'Allhallowgate.'[1] There was also an old chapel of the Virgin called the 'Lady-kirk,' in 'Stammergate,' and there were chapels at the two hospitals and the palace. But there were at first few if any places of worship in the surrounding country, and the most remote of the parishioners had been obliged to repair Ripon. This state of things led to the erection of district chapels by the larger landholders under the sanction of the Chapter, as early as the twelfth century, and of these chapels there were eventually at least sixteen.

---

[1] This church had disappeared, as Leland tells us, long before his visit to Ripon, which took place about 1538. The dates of its erection and demolition are both unknown. In the Chapter-house is preserved a key which has been assigned to the fifteenth century, and which has been thought to have belonged to Allhallows, but it is thought that the church disappeared at an early date.

The parishioners, however, still assembled at Ripon on certain feasts, notably Christmas, Good Friday, Easter, Ascension, Whitsuntide, and the feasts of St. Wilfrid's death (October 12th) and translation (April 24th), to which was added later a feast of his nativity, observed on the Sunday after Lammas Day, and in the parish of Ripon only.[1] On St. Wilfrid's feasts the privilege of sanctuary was extended beyond the mile-limit to all who visited the mother-church, and the penalty for molestation without the limit was £6. On Easter Day all the parishioners received the Communion in the minster,[2] and on that day, on Christmas Day, and on the feast of St. Wilfrid's nativity, the district chaplains attended in their copes. Very picturesque, too, must have been the miracle-plays at Easter, Christmas, and Epiphany; the great fairs; the solemn processions, especially at Rogation-tide, when the relics of the Saint were borne in state by representatives of the greater tenants of the church, and attended by the sanctuary-men carrying staves with banners. It is probable that once a year (perhaps at Whitsuntide) the church was visited by clergy and laity from the whole of that division of the diocese to which Ripon was the mother-church. Such annual visitations were the especial privilege of mother-churches, and were a great source of profit.

Underneath all this pageantry, however, there was much that was unsatisfactory in the internal affairs of the college. In the thirteenth century even more than afterwards, the great difficulty in the working of secular colleges was non-residence. The Canons were often pluralists, or foreigners appointed under pressure from the Pope or the king, who provided in this way for prominent civil servants. A canon would often leave his prebend in the spiritual charge of a vicar engaged by the year, or under the administration of a proctor, or would even farm it out—sometimes to a layman. Sometimes a canon was suspected of being a layman himself, or a married man. The

[1] This Sunday is still called Wilfrid Sunday at Ripon. The Saturday preceding it is the day on which the town commemorates the Saint's return from his first appeal to Rome. The season is regarded as a holiday, and another relic of the nativity festival survives in the fair held on the Thursday after August 2nd.

[2] The Easter Communion has survived till our own day. Within living memory, and at a period when Early Celebrations were not usual, it was celebrated at 7 A.M., and people drove in from the outlying places.

proctors or lessees dismissed or appointed vicars at their pleasure. The prebendal houses fell into disrepair, and in some cases a plot had been assigned, but no house had been built. Some canons at this period resigned their stalls after an extremely short tenure, or changed from one stall to another.

Archbishop Thomas de Corbridge (1299–1303) addressed himself to the reform of these evils. He ordered the Canons to look to their prebendal houses. He tried to control their acceptance of benefices in plurality. He forbade them to farm their prebends to any but brother-canons except with his licence. It was he who gave the prebends their territorial names. Most important of all, he decreed in 1303 that the cure of souls in each prebend was to be entrusted to a vicar-perpetual. The collegiate system was indeed breaking down, and the Vicars henceforth were almost as important a body as the Canons, whom they relieved of all responsibility for the parochial work and the performance of the services. Except the Vicar of Stanwick, they all lived at Ripon, and in 1304 one Nicholas de Bondgate provided them with a common residence, which became known as the Bedern [1] (whence 'Bedern Bank'). The office of *penitentiarius* or of rural dean was often held by one of them. Besides the seven Canons and the six Vicars in Ripon, there were three deacons, three sub-deacons, six thuriblers, and six choristers, and the full officiating staff thus amounted to thirty-one, exclusive of the chantry priests, of whom, however, there were as yet but few.

The successor of Archbishop de Corbridge was an ex-Canon of Ripon, **William Greenfield (Archbishop** 1304–1315). He rebuilt the chapel of the Palace and founded a chantry in it. It was at Ripon that he put forth, with additions of his own, certain rules against clerical abuses which he had borrowed from the diocese of Chichester. He found indeed much to reform. Already the vicariate was becoming demoralized. Vicars and inferior clergy were addicted to shows and sports, to dances and stage-plays. A chaplain invented a gambling game called "ding-thrifts." What wonder that the laity, then, begged at the altars under pretence of being proctors of absent canons, or intruded into the choir during service—a privilege reserved for

---

[1] This word is probably connected with the Anglo-Saxon 'béd,' a prayer (whence 'bedesmen'), and means a 'house of prayer.' In one passage of the records it is rendered in Latin by *proseucha*.

the great ?　And another privilege of rank had been invaded also, for the Archbishop had to direct that only great persons and benefactors were to be buried within the minster. In 1310 two women fought in the graveyard so savagely that it had to be reconsecrated. In his last year the Archbishop had to restrain the proctors of absent canons from acting independently in the administration of the prebends, and from exercising capitular authority.

These internal difficulties, however, were presently forgotten in a new danger from without. Already, in 1298, Archbishop de Newark had called upon the Chapter to assist in providing cavalry for Edward I.'s campaign against John Balliol, King of Scots. The King himself is said to have visited the town in 1300. In 1315 the Chapter had sent a representative to a council held by Archbishop Greenfield at Doncaster to consider the defence of the realm. Since Bannockburn the Scots had been raiding the northern counties, and in 1316 Edward II. ordered Ripon to provide maintenance for Aymer de Valence, Earl of Pembroke, who was to pass through on his way to check the raids. In March 1318 the town sent a contingent to the King's forces, and the money, together with a banner of St. Wilfrid, was provided by **Archbishop William de Melton** (1317–1340). In May of the same year the Scots descended upon Ripon itself. They might have spared the place, for in 1297 it had been the temporary home of the mother of Robert Bruce, now King of Scotland, but no consideration was shown. As there were no town walls, the inhabitants fled to the minster and fortified it. For three days their homes were given over to plunder, and the enemy demanded one thousand marks as the price of a promise not to burn the town altogether. Even the Archbishop urged the townsmen to pay this blackmail lest further damage should be done, but such a sum could not be raised in a moment, and during either this or a subsequent visit the Scots did much damage to the church. The prebends suffered to the extent of over 150 marks, and the hospitals were much crippled. Nor was any satisfaction to be had, save by solemnly excommunicating the enemy on Sundays and festivals. It was probably in consequence of the havoc wrought that in 1322 Parliament, which had been summoned to meet at Ripon, met at York instead.

Thrice again after 1318 were forces levied in the Liberty

against the Scots — in 1327, in 1333, and in 1342, when Edward III. even offered pardon to the sanctuary-men if they would serve.

Meanwhile Archbishop de Melton had been promoting the repair of the minster, a task which included probably the renewal of the spires, the roof, the stained glass, and the wood-work. In 1331–2 he issued some important statutes for the College. Hitherto each Canon (except the Canon of Stanwick) had received an annual dividend out of the Common Fund. Of this fund, a large portion which had always gone to furnish these dividends (or a part of them) was now appropriated exclusively to canons willing to reside. Thus a premium was put upon residence, which was fixed at twelve weeks in the year (not necessarily continuous), and a distinction was admitted between resident and non-resident canons. Again, the Common Fund was now to be charged with the salaries of the Vicars, who had hitherto been precariously paid by the Canons their masters.

Archbishop John de Thoresby (1352–1373) added to the prebend of Studley the two districts of Dacre and Bewerley, and it was probably about this time that the Lady-chapel (now the Library) was built. In 1375 some part of the church was burnt, and in 1396–7 the central spire seems to have been rebuilt. The town had now recovered its prosperity, for in 1405 it became the residence of the Court, when King Henry IV. was driven from Westminster by a plague. The next reign is marked by an improvement in the status of the Vicars. They had been living dispersed over the town, — indeed, their common residence or Bedern is said to have been destroyed by the Scots.

In 1415, therefore, **Archbishop Henry Bowet** (1407–1423), having obtained from Henry V. a charter with a dispensation of the Statute of Mortmain, gave a site out of his manor for a new Bedern; and the vicars themselves, who at this period are commended by both the Archbishop and the King, were at the same time formed into a corporate body having a common seal, and were allowed to elect from their number a Provost. Under this Archbishop there were several instances of canons exchanging their stalls for other benefices. The discipline of the staff seems to have become exceedingly lax by 1439. The church music was neglected. The Mass of Our Lady was not said regularly in the Lady-chapel. The inferior clergy did not study for their examinations, and wore daggers in the Choir. They and the vicars frequented taverns, walked about the nave during service, and absented themselves without leave. The Canons did not attend church in their habits, and the clergy generally indulged in field sports.

Archbishop John Kemp (1426–1452) did what he could to reform these abuses, and effected some improvement (the nature of which is not clear) in the status of the Vicars, who had been badly treated by the Chapter in financial matters. Later in this century a chantry chaplain is found engaging in dishonest trade; priests fight; laymen assault one another in the minster during service. But mediæval morality in general must not be condemned, of course, for a few recorded crimes.

About 1450 the south-east corner of the central tower gave way, and so unsafe was the church that service had to be held in the Lady-kirk. In consequence of this disaster the Canons were obliged to rebuild not only the south and east sides of the tower, but also the east side of the south transept, and eventually part of the south side of the Choir; and it is evident that they would have rebuilt the two remaining sides of the tower, had they not been prevented by the Dissolution. The present rood screen and canopied stalls were put in toward the close of the fifteenth century. In 1502 the Lady-kirk (in which a chantry had been founded in 1392) was handed over by the Chapter to Archbishop Savage, who in turn transferred it to Fountains Abbey. Abbot Huby, intending to make it a colony of Cistercians, rebuilt the east end of it, and enclosed part of its graveyard with a fine stone wall having a strongly-marked base. Of this wall a great part remains in St. Mary-gate. A large doorway in it has been built up. The Lady-kirk itself has vanished long ago.

At this time was begun the greatest architectural enterprise that had been undertaken at Ripon since the twelfth century, namely, the rebuilding of the nave of the minster. The Transitional nave, it was said, had become ruinous through age and storms, but the real motive for its destruction was probably an ambition to enlarge the building. The enlargement of aisleless churches was usually begun by the addition of a single aisle, and that on the north side (since the

UNIVERSITY COLLEGE WINCHESTER
LIBRARY

south was usually the side of the graveyard); but at Ripon the south aisle was built first, perhaps because it was always intended that there should be two aisles—an arrangement which there were no cloisters here to prevent. The work was begun in 1502 or 1503. Delayed by a plague in 1506, it was almost complete, as Leland's *Itinerary* shows,[1] when he visited the town about 1538, but the aisles had not yet been vaulted when the Dissolution came, and had wooden roofs until our own time. Irreparable as is the loss of Archbishop Roger's nave, its successor must surely be placed among the great naves of the Perpendicular period —and it is the latest of them. The work was furthered by **Archbishop Savage** (1501–1507) and by **Cardinal Archbishop Bainbridge** (1508–1514), and two canons must especially be mentioned in connection with it, Andrew Newman, appointed Master of the Fabric in 1502, and **Marmaduke Bradley**, who was paymaster, and who was connected with the repairs after the failure of the central tower, and gave up to the fabric a large portion of his fees for residence. The last work done before the Reformation was probably the rebuilding of the three westernmost bays on the south side of the choir, which had been weakened doubtless by the accident to the central tower.

By this time the church contained nine chantries, namely, those of St. Andrew (founded 1234); of the Holy Trinity *supra summum altare* (1345); of St. John the Evangelist and St. John the Baptist (1364); of St. James (1407–8); of Our Lady 'in the Church' (1408); of St. Thomas of Canterbury (1418); of the Holy Trinity *subtus altare* (1466); of Our Lady 'in the Lady-loft'; and of St. Wilfrid (? 1420). In some of these, other chantries had been merged. There were also four or five chantries in various chapels in the parish. The chantry-chaplains were not strictly on the staff, but helped on Sundays and festivals. As their chantries did not give them sufficient occupation, they sometimes held in addition such offices as that of Proctor of an absent canon, Curator of the Fabric, Sub-Precentor, Sub-Treasurer, or Chamberlain, the holder of this post being the chief financial officer of the community.

[1] It was Walbran, again, who drew attention to Leland's phraseology here.

On the eve of the Reformation the discipline of the staff was again very unsatisfactory, chiefly through the influence of the Treasurer, Canon Christopher Dragley, who employed the vestry clerks on his private business, disposed of chantries prematurely, and encouraged the Vicars, who were now living dispersed, to be insubordinate. It was the custom for choir and clergy to adjourn after Prime to the Chapter-house, where the martyrology for the day was read and notices were given out. Here, too, once a week sat the Chapter Court. But Dragley was able to hinder all this by keeping the door locked. From 1533 to 1539 he was Treasurer, Canon Residentiary, and President of the Chapter, and the general laxity was largely due to this concentration of authority in the hands of one bad man through non-residence. The case of Dragley drew several decrees from **Archbishop Edward Lee** (1531–1544) :—that no vicar should be appointed without the consent of a majority in Chapter ; that the Chapter seal must be kept by three people ; that one canon must no longer form a quorum (as hitherto) in the Chapter Court, and as a question had arisen whether the powers of the Chapter were not entirely vested in the canons-resident,[1] it was laid down that the latter were indeed competent to dispose of certain chantries and other offices, and to exercise the Chapter's spiritual jurisdiction, but that in most other matters the whole body must be consulted. As most of them were always absent, this means, perhaps, that they were represented in Chapter by their proctors. There is an instance in 1546 of the Vicars, chantry priests, and deacons being allowed to take part in a Chapter meeting.

An attack on relics was begun in 1538, and it was probably about this date that the shrine of St. Wilfrid was destroyed. In 1539 came the suppression of Fountains Abbey, the abbot who surrendered it being no other than Marmaduke Bradley. He had been Abbot since 1536, holding his canonry at Ripon at the same time, and after the suppression of the Abbey, he became once more a power at Ripon. As sole residentiary in 1544, 1545, and 1546, he appears to have used his influence well, and played a prominent part in the last architectural opera-

---

[1] The Canon of Stanwick was always in Ripon, but was not considered technically a canon-resident. Perhaps he was not entitled to the special fees for residence. He had, however, full capitular rights. These had been denied to him by Dragley, but were now restored by the Archbishop.

tions before the Dissolution. The old system of sanctuary, suited only to times when the State was weak, seems to have died out about this period. In 1545 came an Act for the dissolution of chantries and hospitals. As 'Supreme Head of the Church' Henry VIII. renewed the visitatorial authority of the Archbishops, and both he and Edward VI. confirmed the ecclesiastical jurisdiction of the Chapter. But the end was imminent. In 1547 the College was dissolved,[1] and its revenues were annexed to the Duchy of Lancaster. There had been attached to the church for centuries a **Grammar School**, for which the Chapter had claimed a monopoly of education within the Parish and Liberty, forbidding in 1468 the establishment of any other school without their special licence. This ancient seminary was apparently dissolved, and a new grammar school independent of the church was founded by Edward VI., whose benefaction was completed by Mary, the endowment being provided from the revenues of four of the late chantries. There had also been a Song-school, but it was perhaps merely a room in which boys of the Grammar School were trained to be choristers. Out of the confiscated revenues one or more clergy were paid to minister to the parish, but under Mary the old state of things was in some measure brought back. There was once more a Chamberlain, whose accounts show much the same items as do those of his mediæval predecessors, and the old religion was restored; indeed, there were six altars in the church.

Under Elizabeth there was a return to the arrangement of Edward, the clergy (now as many as five in number) being denominated vicars. Archbishop Sandys (1577–1588), Lord Burleigh, Richard Hooker, Moses Fowler (afterwards the first Dean), and others tried to bring about the establishment of a theological college in the Bedern, and an increase of the endowments of the church, but in vain. The town must have lost all favour in 1569, by taking part in the Rising in the North. It was visited by the rebel earls of Northumberland and Westmorland, many of the townsmen and local gentry joining them, and for the last time the minster witnessed the celebration of the Mass. On the collapse of the rebellion, a number of those who had taken up arms were hanged at

---

[1] If the Ripon hospitals were dissolved they were re-established, for they are still fulfilling their purpose.

Ripon in sight of their homes, and the church suffered much damage from the Queen's soldiery, who stripped the lead from the roof. Like the Pilgrimage of Grace in 1536, this Rising was a protest against the Reformation, and the records of Archbishop Young (1561–1568), and of the Court of High Commission (1580), show that the people of Ripon still clung to the old religion. The pillage of Henry and Edward had no doubt destroyed most of the ornaments of the church, but some still remained or had been renewed under Mary, and the clergy displayed a marked reluctance in removing them; 'Images,' even when removed, were concealed in private houses. One vicar named Thomas Blackburne had continued the old practice of holding churchings in the Lady-chapel, and was ordered publicly to renounce this error, as well as that of having left "that olde, abhominable, and supersticious vawte called the Wilfride's nedle [1] and the alter therein" undefaced. One townsman is punished for having taken part in the Mass during the late Rising. The clergy generally were unclerical in dress and lax in their performance of the reformed services, which the parishioners showed a corresponding unwillingness to attend, while the old fasts and festivals were not wholly given up.

The Chapter revived.—On the accession of **James I.** a second futile attempt was made to obtain for Ripon a theological college.[2] The influence, however, of the queen, **Anne of Denmark**, gained from the king a greater boon, and in 1604 he re-established the Chapter. Under the new constitution there were six prebendaries, and for the first time a Dean. Much of the old endowments was restored, but the new stalls could not be identified with the old territorial prebends, and were therefore distinguished as 'the first stall,' 'the second stall,' and so on. After 1607 the Prebendaries were empowered to elect a Sub-Dean. The cure of souls was discharged by two vicars, and the choir was composed of six lay-clerks and six choristers. The parish remained a Peculiar. The spiritual jurisdiction of the Chapter and the Archbishop had been somewhat restricted by the Reformation, and the secular jurisdiction of the Liberty—especially in criminal cases—had been partly transferred to the king's itinerant justices.

---

[1] *I.e.*, the Saxon crypt.
[2] The project is being realized in our own day.

he South Prospect of ᵞᵉ Ripponensis eccl conven
onuentuall Church of Rippon) facies authens.

Maneat virs:
Tollatur abutus
Iohaes Rothworth
Arm:

D King delin et sculp

RIPON MINSTER ANTERIOR TO 1660.

Note.—This representation much resembles that engraved on the old communion plate. As a view of Ripon Minster, it

The Archbishop, however, still retained some criminal jurisdiction and also his 'Court Military,' which, strange to say, came to hear civil cases. During the latter half of the fifteenth century the secular cases heard by the Chapter had been chiefly cases of debt, and under the new constitution they were authorized to hold a court, which was called the Canon Fee Court, for cases of debt and other civil cases. Some obscurity exists as to the mediæval relation of the Archbishop to the town. There was, of course, a town council, and its president the Wakeman[1] (an official peculiar to Ripon) had charge of what would now be called the town police. The ancient town bridges (of which only one remains) were under the charge of the Archbishop. During the sixteenth century the borough constitution had been the subject of disputes, in which Cardinal Wolsey had been concerned in 1517 and Archbishop Hutton in 1598. James I. therefore now granted a new Charter, under which the Wakeman became a Mayor; and henceforth the borough had also an independent court of its own. The dissolution of the Chapter in 1547, coming as it did upon the decay of the manufacture of woollen cloth, had been a great blow to the prosperity of the inhabitants,[2] and it was no wonder that when James visited the town in 1617 he received an ovation.

In 1625 a plague, such as had not occurred here since 1546, prevented the country folk from approaching the minster, and obliged them to have their children baptized in the fields.

[1] *I.e.*, the watchman, or setter of the watch. The town motto is, "Except the Lord keep the city, the *Wakeman* waketh in vain." After 1598 a horn was blown every evening to denote the setting of the watch. If any house was robbed between horn-blowing and sunrise, compensation could be claimed from the town. To support this system a small tax was levied on each house-door, and if a house had two doors it paid more, as being more liable to be robbed. A relic of the system still survives. Every night a horn is blown thrice before the Mayor's door at 9 P.M. and thrice at the Market Cross afterwards. The ancient horn of the Wakeman (which appears on the city arms) is still worn by the Sergeant-at-mace in civic processions.

[2] Since then, however, another industry had arisen—the manufacture of spurs, for which Ripon became famous, and James was presented with a pair. This industry did not die out till the end of the last century, and a spur is still the crest of the city. The manufacture of saddle-trees, which flourished here in the sixteenth century, is still carried on.

C

Several changes in the surroundings of the church took place at this time. The Bedern, with its quadrangle, hall, and chapel, had been demolished by 1625, in which year the Deanery was erected, perhaps upon its site. Of the old prebendal houses some had been sold, or let; others, perhaps, were occupied by the Prebendaries of the new foundation. In 1629 the ancient Palace, which stood to the north of the minster and west of the Deanery, was turned into a poor-house. The town (and doubtless the minster) was visited in 1633 by Charles I. on his way to his coronation at Edinburgh.[1]   A few years later he was to pass through again, a captive on his way to Holmby House.

Ripon had escaped the Wars of the Roses, but it was not unscathed by the Great Rebellion, for in 1643 it was occupied by Sir Thomas Mauleverer, a Parliamentary officer, whose soldiery broke into the minster and shattered the magnificent glass in the great east window, and doubtless much other glass besides.   At the end of the war the manorial rights were sold to Lord Fairfax, and the Chapter was again dissolved, "one who called himself Dr. Richardson" being "appointed to preach in the minster by the Parliament, tho' in all probability he was never in any Orders, Presbyterian or Episcopal."[2]   The Chapter was revived at the Restoration, but all its members were new save one.

In the same year (1660) the central spire, which had been injured by lightning in 1593, fell through the roof, wrecking many of the beautiful canopies of the stalls.   The damage to the choir and other parts of the church, estimated at £6000, was repaired with money raised under a brief from Charles II., but the spire was never rebuilt, and in 1664, to avoid any further catastrophe, the western spires, though sound, were deliberately removed.[3]   The place of the spires

---

[1] In 1640 he was at war with the Scots for their opposition to episcopacy, and it was at Ripon that the disgraceful negotiations were begun, by which a sum of £850 a day was to be paid to maintain their invading army, pending a more permanent settlement.   The house in which the 'Treaty of Ripon' was negotiated stood near Ailcy Hill, and disappeared about the beginning of the century.   Charles is said to have visited the town four times altogether.

[2] Walker's "Sufferings of the Clergy," quoted in *Surtees Soc.*, Vol. 78. There is a tablet to Richardson's wife in the south Choir-aisle.

[3] The following is probably the true version of a story that is told in

was ill supplied by the erection of battlements and pinnacles, which were renewed in 1797.

It was perhaps at this period that the west gate of the precincts was pulled down—a mediæval structure which contained at least seven rooms, and which stood at the bottom of Kirkgate. The graveyard in the middle ages contained a cross, at which a service was held on Palm Sunday; also, possibly, a mortuary chapel and a well associated with St. Wilfrid—(not, of course, the St. Wilfrid's well which now fills the public baths). Of these things there is now not a trace, save, perhaps, the stump of the cross, near the south wall of the nave. Nor are there any undoubted remains of the mediæval wall which enclosed the precincts, except the fragment with an archway in it, which still forms the southern entrance. The mediæval prisons, which belonged respectively to the Archbishop and the Chapter, have long vanished, as has also that which appertained to the Court of Canon Fee, but there is a Liberty prison of some age in 'Stammergate.' Most of the archiepiscopal palace had disappeared by 1830, but there was still a portion which was used as the court-house of the Liberty. In that year this was pulled down, and the present court-house was built upon the site. A memory of the Palace survives in 'Hall Yard,' and there still remains what is, perhaps, a remnant of the actual fabric, in the shape of an old cottage with an external staircase, which stands behind the wall to the west of the public garden that fronts the north side of the church. In the above-mentioned wall is an Early English doorway, with a dripstone adorned with the nailhead moulding. The door has a flat-arched wooden frame, the spandrels of which are carved with *fleurs-de-lys*, while the wooden tympanum above has Perpendicular panelling. This doorway is not, perhaps, a relic of the Palace. It is not in its original position, and indeed is said to have come originally from St. Mary Magdalene's Hospital. Several of the old houses adjoining the Cathedral on the south side, and along St. Agnes-gate, may possibly have been inhabited by the

connection with their demolition. One of the workmen had been hoisted by means of a pulley, and was being held aloft by his comrades below, when he spied some coursing in progress on Bondgate Green. Seeing the hare well away and the dogs straining in the leash, he shouted "Let go!" And his comrades below did.

Prebendaries of the Second Collegiate foundation, but the stone-roofed house adjoining Bondgate Green Bridge is the only one in Ripon which can be identified with a mediæval prebend —that of Thorp, and even here the existing fabric can scarcely be pre-Reformation. St. John's Hospital,[1] whose inmates for several centuries have been women, was unfortunately rebuilt in 1869, but the modern chapel (served by one of the cathedral clergy) retains a bell of 1663. The old Grammar School,[2] which stood at the foot of the steps from St. Agnes-gate to the Minster, has been pulled down since 1872.

Meanwhile the Minster itself had been undergoing restoration—in 1829 and the following years at the hands of Blore, when upwards of £3000 were spent, and from 1862 to 1870 at the hands of Sir G. Gilbert Scott, and at a cost of about £30,000.

From the eighth century up to 1836 Ripon had been in the diocese of York. In that year was created the modern diocese of Ripon, and the church thus attained to cathedral rank. It had, however, always had some pretension to that rank, not merely as a mother-church but because (up to 1836) the Archbishops had their throne in the choir; indeed, it is styled a cathedral in documents of 1537 and 1546. The diocese is composed of parts of Yorkshire taken from the sees of York and Chester, and included Wakefield, Leeds, Bradford, Halifax and Huddersfield, until in 1888 a portion including Halifax and Huddersfield was taken away to form part of a new diocese of Wakefield. There are three archdeaconries: those of Richmond, Ripon, and Craven. The first is a survival, in a diminished form, of the ancient archdeaconry of the same name; the others are modern; the last is the only one which is held without a canonry. In accordance with the Act of 1840, the Sub-Deanery has been suppressed, the Prebendaries have been reduced to four, and their style has been changed to that of Canons. In 1841, provision was made for the appointment of

---

[1] For the other hospitals, the 'Thorp' house, and other old buildings still standing, see Chap. IV.

[2] Ripon Grammar School has produced an Archbishop of York, Matthew Hutton (one of the two of that name who held the office from 1595 to 1606 and from 1749 to 1757 respectively: the latter Hutton became Archbishop of Canterbury); also Beilby Porteous, Bishop of London (1776–1787), and Dr. William Stubbs, late Bishop of Oxford.

Canons honorary. There is also a precentor, and three other clergy who act as minor canons, and assist him in discharging the cure of souls—for though the huge mediæval parish has been gradually divided into many, the greater portion of the city itself is still served from the cathedral church. The choir is composed of six lay-clerks and twelve choristers. There was as late as 1890 a Choir-school, but most of the present choristers come from Jepson's Hospital—a charity which was founded in 1672, in Water Skellgate, and the old buildings of which were pulled down in 1878.

There are still some relics of the ancient jurisdictions of the Chapter and the Archbishop. Though the secular jurisdiction has been gradually reduced by legislation to the scope of Quarter and Petty Sessions, the Liberty has Quarter Sessions of its own, and its justices are still nominated by the Archbishop, while his Court Military survived at any rate into the nineteenth century. A copyhold court, called the Canon Fee Court, is also still held by the Chapter. As regards ecclesiastical jurisdiction, the mediæval right of the Chapter to hear testamentary and matrimonial cases (which were not taken away from the ecclesiastical courts till 1857) probably survived at least until the abolition of the Peculiar. Peculiars, with but one or two exceptions, had ceased to exist by 1850, and Ripon, once exempt from archidiaconal authority, is now itself an archdeaconry. The Bishop of Ripon has, of course, his Consistory court, which is held at the Cathedral.

In ending this account of one of the most venerable of English churches, it is worth while to remark that, of the four mother-churches of the old diocese of York, Ripon is the only one besides York Cathedral itself which still has a collegiate foundation.

Ronald P. Jones, Photo.]

THE CATHEDRAL FROM THE SOUTH-EAST.

Ronald P. Jones, Photo.]

THE WEST DOORWAYS.

CHAPTER II.

THE EXTERIOR.

BUILT upon the verge of a slope, along whose base the Skell hurries eastwards under many bridges to join the Ure among the meadows a half-mile below the town, Ripon Cathedral stands unusually well.[1] Of general views the two best, perhaps, are to be had from the wooden bridge by Bondgate Green, and from the south-east gate of the graveyard. Unfortunately lack of funds prevented Sir Gilbert Scott from raising the roofs of nave and transept to their original pitch; but what most injures the general effect is the lowness of the central tower, which is no higher than those at the west end. This fault, however, must have been far less noticeable when all three towers were crowned with lofty spires. And, even as it stands, the exterior of Ripon is dignified and not unworthy of its commanding site. The size of the clearstorey windows, the

---

[1] The name Ripon comes probably from the Latin *ripa*, "a river's bank." Bede uses a form "Inrhypum," which arose perhaps out of *in ripis*. The derivation *Uri pons* has been generally abandoned.

severity of the transept, the obvious variety of style and date throughout the building—these are the features that strike the observer most forcibly.

Several kinds of material have been employed. Up to almost the end of the thirteenth century the builders used a coarse gritstone such as is found five miles to the south-west at Brimham Rocks, and also a finer gritstone or sandstone that may have come from Hackfall. After that date they built with magnesian limestone, brought partly, perhaps, from near York, but chiefly, it would seem, from Quarry Moor, a mile south of the city. At the last restoration the older parts were repaired with Hackfall stone, and the later parts with limestone from Quarry Moor and Monkton Moor, and so extensive were the repairs needed on the exterior, that the church somewhat belies, by its appearance, its real antiquity.

The most picturesque approach is from High St. Agnes-gate by a flight of steps, which ascend through an old arch to an avenue of limes that leads up to the south door; but it is better, perhaps, that the survey should begin at the west end.

The West Front was doubtless the object of two indulgences, issued respectively by Archbishop de Gray in 1233 and by Pope Alexander IV. in 1258, and was therefore erected just before or during the struggle between Henry III. and Simon de Montfort, in the best period of the Early English style.

The height of the gable is said to be 103 feet, and that of the towers 110 feet, and the front is divided by the string-courses into four stages. In the central compartment the lowest stage is approached by three steps, and is filled by three door-ways, set in a thickening of the wall, and surmounted by gables finished with crosses. The central entrance, higher, more widely splayed, and more deeply recessed than the others, has five orders and five triple shafts in the jamb, while they have three orders and three shafts, the innermost of which is triple and the others single. As usual in this style, the shafts are detached and not worked on the stones of the jamb. The mouldings of the capitals are carried through the jamb from end to end, and on the front of the piers between the arch-ways is a curious moulding which resembles an undercut roll set up on end, and which has a capital as if it were a shaft. In the arches the mouldings are chiefly rounds and hollows: many of the former are filleted, and some of the latter are filled with the dog-tooth (an ornament peculiar to this style), which is more profusely employed in the central arch than in the others. The terminations of the dripstones are foliated and stand out detached. The central gable is adorned with a square panel of foliage, and either of the others with a sunk foliated quatrefoil, and between the gables are spouts issuing from the heads of animals. It is worthy of remark that all three doors open into the nave ; for as a rule when a church has three west doors, two of them open into the aisles.[1] The wooden doors in these and all the doorways of the church are of considerable age, and those in the central archway here bear the date 1673 in nails.

Above the doors is a tier of five lancet windows, and above these another tier, also of five, which diminish in height toward the sides, the last window at either end being, however, as high as the tier below. These tiers occupy the whole width of the compartment. Above them, again, is a group of three small lancets graduated to the gable and placed very high, with a string-course below them. These serve to light the space between the internal and external roofs. In all this work the detail is of the very best : the various arches are richly moulded and supported by clusters of engaged shafts, which in the two great tiers are banded at about half their height, and the dog-tooth ornament is everywhere employed profusely. The lower tier is the more elaborate—its mouldings more numerous, its shafts more richly clustered, its capitals covered with foliage ; and between the second and third lancets from the right there is a small niche with a toothed edge and the remains of a figure. At either end of the two tiers an ornament not unlike the ball-flower of the Decorated style is carried up the jamb, and a bold corbel-table runs up the sides of the gable, under the apex of which there is a trefoil panel, while the whole is crowned by an elaborate cross.

In the towers the lowest of the four stages is relieved by a little arcade of six trefoiled arches, with detached shafts, fluted capitals, and dripstones not trefoiled and terminating in heads. Each of the three upper stages is occupied by three tall lancets, of which that in the centre, higher and broader than the others, is pierced and (except in the belfry) glazed. In their enrich-

---

[1] The reason of the peculiarity here is the unusual width of the nave. (*See below*, p. 44.)

ment these arcades resemble the windows of the central compartment. The second stage is not quite so high here in the towers as it is there, and the level of the string-course above is consequently broken. The third stage, taller than the second, reaches to the springing of the gable. The fourth, taller than the third, rises somewhat above the gable cross, and the shafts of the lancets are twice banded, while above are two circular

Ronald P. Jones, Photo.]

VIEW FROM THE NORTH-WEST.

panels, which on the north tower are raised and contain quatrefoils, but on the south tower are sunk and contain trefoils. On the other faces of these towers the arches are not so richly moulded, and the shafts are single and also detached, except in the uppermost stage of the north tower, where they are engaged and filleted. As the second stage does not descend so low upon the western face as upon the other faces, the string-course below it, after passing round the corners of the façade, is stopped, and when it is resumed it passes above the sill of the arcade, being carried round the little plinths of the shafts. All the string-courses, it will be noticed, are enriched with the nailhead moulding. The buttresses rise to the parapets without diminishing in breadth or projection—an early feature, and three large rolls or beads are worked upon their edge. Those that flank the portal have each a large niche at the bottom, with engaged shafts, and the head and dripstone trefoiled. At the corners of the façade, where the staircases are, the buttresses are triple. The original corbel-table, surmounted by a row of dog-tooth ornament, remains at the top of the towers, but the battlements and pinnacles have been put up since the removal of the spires in 1664, and were renewed in 1797.

The bells, ten in number, are in the south tower. Of the mediæval peal, which consisted of six bells, the largest, known as the *Klank Knoll*, was made in 1379 at York, and perhaps hung in the north tower; while some of the others seem to have been made in Ripon in 1391. They were all recast in 1761 by Lester & Pack of London, after which there were eight. Two of these (Nos. 4 and 7) were recast in 1866 by Warner of London, and two new bells (Nos. 1 and 2), by Shaw of Bradford, have been added since 1890. The ninth bell is rung every evening at nine for the curfew. The mediæval clock, mentioned in 1379, has long vanished; another was put up in 1723; the present clock (by Thwaites of Clerkenwell) dates from 1808.

The whole front has been much restored by Sir Gilbert Scott, especially the doorways and the towers. The latter were badly cracked through settlement (due partly to the fact that in either tower one of the sides is older than the rest),[1] but, as Sir Gilbert himself declared, they are once more strong enough to bear spires, and it is to be hoped that the hint will some day be taken. The more the west front of Ripon is studied, the more it becomes apparent how much thought has been expended upon it. Yet as a work of art it is perplexing. To some it will appear beautiful as a design; to others its excellence of detail will be its only commendation, and they will complain that the tiers of windows are wider than the gable, that there is a disproportion between the little arcade in the lowest stage of the towers and the great lancets in the upper stages, that the height of the latter makes the towers appear top-heavy, that the whole façade lacks projection and

[1] This will be explained in Chapter III.

depth of shade, and that there is too much glass. Some dis-
satisfaction was felt, as the Fabric Rolls indicate, in 1379,
when masons were employed to divide each of the large
windows into two lights with a quatrefoil above.[1] The mullions
and quatrefoils remained till our own day, when they were
removed by Sir Gilbert Scott, whose action the present state of
expert opinion on restoration would severely condemn.

The Nave. North Side.—By being rebuilt with the
addition of aisles, the nave became as wide as the west front.
Its width is 87 feet internally and nearly 100 feet externally,
and it is the widest nave in England after York, Winchester,
Chichester, and St. Paul's. The date of the rebuilding is indicated by a Chapter minute of 1502, which alludes to the
onus canonicis modo impositum super reædificationem navis. The
Fabric Rolls mention the purchase of stone in 1503, and the
roofing of some "new work" in 1505, while a will of 1508
requires the testator's body to be buried in "the new work of
the College Church." These are doubtless references to the
south side, which is evidently the older and bears internally
the arms of Archbishop Savage (1501–1507). Again, an indulgence of 1512, by Archbishop Bainbridge (1508–1514),
alluding to the demolition of the old nave as then complete,
suggests that the north wall had been left standing till then,
and the laying of the foundation of the north aisle, which
bears his arms, is mentioned in the Roll for 1512–13. It
appears from the Rolls that the main roof was up by 1520–21.
Lastly, Leland's allusion to "the body of the Chirch of late
dayes made of a great Widnesse" shows that the main part
of the work was finished at any rate by about 1538.[2]

The nave is divided—east of the towers—into six bays, of
which the easternmost is narrower than the rest, to answer to
a fragment of the old nave preserved within. The plinth is
considerably higher than that of the west front.

On the north side, the six buttresses project 5 feet at the
base and rise to the parapet in two stages, which are crowned
by gables. These gables have their sides curved inwards and
are adorned with crockets and finials, the latter being attached
to the front of the gable, while grotesques project from the
angles. The windows are of three lights, and are rather acutely
pointed and deeply set for such late work, and their arches

---

[1] See illustration, p. 17.   [2] This was pointed out by Walbran.

are well moulded, a broad hollow running up the sides. As is often the case in late work, there are no sub-arches in the tracery, and the mullions are carried up through the head. The easternmost of these windows is of two lights, and has a transom in the tracery, and the westernmost is shortened to allow of a doorway of four-centred form beneath. Below the sills runs a string-course, which rises to pass over the door. The parapet is battlemented, not for military purposes but for ornament, and at intervals are the beginnings of panelled pinnacles, set diagonally and partially embedded in the battlements. The clearstorey has no pilasters or buttresses, but where it joins the west tower a projecting strip of masonry may be seen half imbedded in the Early English work and half in the Perpendicular. This is, without doubt, the upper part of one of the buttresses of the old nave.

The clearstorey windows are actually larger than those of the aisle below, and are again rather acutely pointed for late work. They are of five lights, and the two mullions in the middle are carried up through the head, but a sub-arch comprises the two outer lights on either side. The last window eastwards is of three lights, is shorter than the rest, and has several transoms in the tracery. In the parapet, the coping is not carried down the sides of the battlements as it is on the aisles, and the rudimentary pinnacles spring from grotesque corbels at the string-course, with a plain corbel at the side of each to carry the water-spout.

The Central Tower. North and West Sides.—

The central tower of Ripon is probably unique among towers in being divided vertically between two different styles of architecture. Its north and west sides are Archbishop Roger's work,[1] but the other sides are Perpendicular, having been rebuilt after the collapse of the south-east angle. Seen from the northwest, however, it presents much the same appearance now as in the twelfth century, and either side displays a pair of round-headed windows, with the weathering of the original roof rising high between them and (on the west face) cutting off their corners. The windows have a shaft in the jamb, and the abacus of the capitals is continued round the tower as a

---

[1] The Transitional or Transition-Norman work at Ripon probably was not all erected during Roger's lifetime, but all of it will, in these pages, be associated with his name.

string, but interrupted by the buttresses and weatherings, as is also another string below the sills. In the windows of the north side there is a space or tympanum over the inner arch. Each corner of the tower was strengthened by a pair of flat buttresses, with one shaft at the corner itself and another at the inner side of either buttress, and with the shafts banded half way up and again near the top. These buttresses are received in an overhanging corbel-table, above which runs a hollow moulding, filled with dog-tooth ornament of a large size and continued round the projections that serve for gargoyles. The use of this Early English ornament in a scheme which might otherwise be pure Norman affords a good instance of the Transitional character of the work. The battlements are later.

The North Transept, with the three adjacent bays of the choir, gives some idea of the external appearance of Archbishop Roger's church.[1] The date of the beginning of the work ascribed to him is placed within his lifetime (1154–1181) by his own words quoted in Chapter I. The transept is divided by the string-courses into four stages, and has a very massive plinth which is lower than that of the nave, thus expressing the slope of the ground. The west wall is shorter than the east and has two bays only, but south of the second bay, and separated from it by a flat pilaster, is a narrow space, along the top of which are the remains of a cornice : the two bays proper are separated by a recessed buttress of some projection. One round-headed window, divided by a mullion, appears in the second stage ; and in the fourth stage are two plain, round-headed windows, not subdivided. The original corbel-table remains above, but it is surmounted by a (probably) fourteenth century battlemented parapet, which is returned over the central buttress, forming a square turret, which has a (renewed) gargoyle below it, and is pierced with a cross. The buttresses at the north-west corner of the transept, where is a staircase, are clustered and rise to the top of the wall, and like most Norman buttresses, and some of Early English date (as in the west front), they do not diminish as they ascend. The large buttress on the west side of this

---

[1] Upon a modern Chapter seal there is what is possibly meant for a representation of Roger's church, with western towers, three spires, and no aisles. The seal is a reproduction of another of the time of James I., which may have been reproduced from a third of earlier date.

corner has two carved stones built into it at the height of about eighteen feet from the ground. They are covered with patterns resembling the knots so often found on ancient crosses, and are of especial interest as being possibly survivals of the church built by St. Wilfrid.[1] It is noticeable that the

first string-course is the only one which is not carried round the buttresses at this corner. A recessed buttress of the same type separates the end of the transept from that of an aisle which is thrown out from its eastern side.

The lowest stage of this north elevation is blank save for a rather interesting doorway set in a thickening of the wall near the western corner. In this doorway the innermost arch is of unusual form—a trefoil resting on corbels —and its edges are left square and plain. Over it is a semicircular arch of three orders with three detached shafts in either jamb, and as usual throughout almost all

Ronald P. Jones, Photo.]

DOORWAY, NORTH TRANSEPT.

Archbishop Roger's work, the arch has the edge-roll between hollows (here on every order), the shafts are detached, their bases round upon square, and their capitals square-topped, with the edge of the abacus hollowed. The capitals here are enriched with good foliage of a rather classical type.

[1] For the origin and meaning of this knotwork, so often found in these islands on ancient crosses, and for its value as an illustration of the possible connection of Saxon architecture with the Comacine Guild of Italy, see *The Cathedral Builders*, by Leader Scott, pp. 82–99, and p. 145.

In the stage above are three round-headed windows with a shaft in either jamb and foliage on the capitals. Each of these windows, like that on the west side, and several in the other transept, has been divided by a mullion into two lights, presumably in the fourteenth century.[1] The third stage, which corresponds to the triforium within, is blank here as on the west side, and in the fourth stage are three round-headed windows, plainly recessed and chamfered. The gable, on which stands a plain cross, has been lowered, as is shown by the weathering on the tower, and its sides, after descending, take an upward turn to meet the corners. It is flanked by two lofty square turrets, which have been compared with those on the west front of Tewkesbury. They have a shaft at each angle, are pierced on each face with two round-headed openings under a round arch, with a string below running round the turret, and are surmounted by pyramidal stone caps ending in pommels and having a rude pinnacle at each corner. The end of the aisle is set back, and displays a window like the three above the door, but without the dividing mullion ; and above this a round-headed niche, doubtless once a window that lighted the space over the aisle-vault ; while a round arch over this niche, and a little pointed arch on the buttress adjacent westwards, carry a curious thickening of the masonry above. The arrangement of the windows here breaks the continuity of the first string-course, which, after crossing the main elevation, has to be stopped and resumed at a lower level in order to pass beneath the windows of the aisle. At the corner of the latter are more clustered buttresses, terminating below the parapet, and above them rises a plain gabled pinnacle (an addition, probably, of the fourteenth century), while another buttress, rising from the inclined coping of the aisle-wall, runs up the clearstorey.

The east side of the aisle has two more buttresses like those at the corner, and consists of two bays, each containing a window like that at the end. It is hard to say whether the moulded string or cornice below the parapet is original, but the gargoyle which juts from it and the parapet itself, with its

---

[1] This was the case with all the windows of both transepts—in the lower tier at any rate—until the last restoration. The reason why Sir Gilbert Scott has left or renewed the mullions in some of the windows is probably that he did not wish to disturb the memorial glass.

cruciform piercings, are not earlier than the fourteenth century. The roofs of the aisles in both transepts and in the choir have been lowered, and it has been suggested that this was done at the time when the Minster was fortified against the Scots, in order to afford better standing-room for armed men,[1] and the various battlements on choir and transepts were probably erected for the same occasion. Here the round arches of the triforium have been built up, and the clearstorey harmonizes with the more elaborate scheme of the choir. The wall is divided into three bays by flat pilasters received in the cornice, and each bay contains a round arch, pierced and glazed, between two lower and narrower pointed arches, all resting on single detached shafts. Between the buttresses runs a corbel-table, supporting a battlemented parapet of Decorated character, in which the merlons are of great width in proportion to the embrasures—an early feature—and have the usual cruciform piercings, so splayed at the back as to leave no doubt that they were really intended for the use of archers. The three gargoyles below have been renewed, and none of the gargoyles on choir or transepts are earlier, perhaps, than the Decorated period.

The Choir. North Side.—Here the three westernmost bays of the aisle and clearstorey respectively are Archbishop Roger's work. Two flat pilaster-buttresses rise out of the slope of the plinth and run up the aisle-wall, each terminating short of the parapet in two sets-off close together. The level of the window-sills was the same here as in the transept, but the string-course has been broken in the Decorated period by the insertion of three slender windows, each having two lights with a quatrefoil above. Above the windows comes the moulded string or cornice continued from the transept, and above this the pierced merlons of the Decorated battlement are again very broad in proportion to the embrasures. Instead of being built up, the exposed arches of the triforium have here been glazed. The clearstorey resembles that of the transept, but the corbel table is surmounted here by a slope, on which rest two large gargoyles (renewed), and instead of a Decorated battlement there is a plain coping.

The last three bays of the clearstorey and the last two of the aisle are Decorated work, probably of the end of the

[1] The suggestion was made by Mr. Francis Bond.

D

thirteenth century, and here the level of the plinth is again lowered to suit the slope of the ground. In the aisle the two bays are separated from the rest and from each other by buttresses having a projection of 8 feet. Either of these buttresses is crowned by a gable having a finial, and is surmounted by a tall square pinnacle to receive the thrust of a flying buttress that spans the aisle; and either pinnacle has its sides panelled and gabled, a head at each corner, and five finials. The two last aisle-windows are larger than those in the western bays, but have much the same tracery. They have, however, a thick shaft worked on the stones of the jamb, and a large keeled round on the edge of the arch, and there is no dripstone. Below them is a small string-course, which is carried round the east end. The string or cornice above them is made to match that on the western portion of the aisle, but in the battlement the merlons are of merely ordinary width. In the clearstorey the wall is considerably set back from the Transitional bays, and the three windows are very elaborate. Their arches are richly moulded and acutely pointed, the springing-line being rather low down. Each window is divided into four lights, comprised under two sub-arches, either of which contains a circle enclosing a trefoil, while above, in the head of the window, is a large circle with five trefoils radiating from its centre. The dripstones end in heads. A moulded string-course, with gargoyles, runs below the parapet, which is a continuation of the plain coping on the western bays.

From this point it will be best to return to the west front, and proceed along the south side of the Cathedral.

The Nave. South Side.—This side is architecturally superior to the other, and differs from it greatly in detail. The plinth, which is very massive, rises even higher above that of the west front here than it does there, and the buttresses project over 8 feet at the base and are of three stages, and the gables on these have their sides straight, their eaves everywhere continued to the wall, and their corners enriched with heads, but on the second stage only. In the two easternmost buttresses the lowest stage has heads also, and in the last buttress eastwards this stage, for some unexplained reason, is twice as broad as the others, and has an ogee gable. On all gables the crockets are large, and the finials, which here stand upon the apex, are huge and very boldly executed; while the rudimentary pinnacles are thicker here than on the north side and more detached from the parapet. The wall is thickened up to the windows, below which there is a set-off, and the windows themselves are so moulded as to seem set in heavy frames, and are much less acutely pointed than in the other aisle, their arches approaching the 'drop' form. The rather clumsy mullions are carried up through the head, but branch out to form arches over the side lights, and are reduced in thickness above the branching point; and in the head there is a transom, except in the narrow easternmost window. Though the aisles differ so much, the clearstorey is much the same on this side as on the other, and again one of Archbishop Roger's buttresses is visible, imbedded between the Perpendicular walling and the west tower. The height of his roof is indicated by the weathering on the central tower and by the west gable, and the sixteenth century roof was probably not lower, for the central tower shows high weatherings of the latter period also; but the pitch had been lowered before the last restoration, and Sir Gilbert Scott was unable to raise it to the full height. It is to be hoped that the raising may yet be accomplished, and that lead may be substituted for slate.

The South Transept, all but its eastern side, is mainly Archbishop Roger's work. The plinth is altogether lower not only than that of the nave, and even of the west front, but also than that of the other transept, and the architecture thus expresses the downward slope of the ground from north to south as well as from west to east. Here, as in the nave, the buttresses have a greater projection than on the north side of the church, as if the ground here were more liable to settle. As this transept bears a general resemblance to the other, it will be best to note only the points in which they differ. In the west wall the window in the second stage has no mullion, the innermost buttress is of the same type as its next neighbour, and the parapet is returned over all the buttresses, thus forming three 'turrets,' of which that nearest to the nave rests partially on a large corbel. The staircase at the south-west corner terminates at the top in a square turret with a pyramidal stone cap.

In the south elevation the doorway is very elaborate. The opening is of the form sometimes called the shouldered arch, a square lintel (which, curiously enough, is not one stone) resting

UNIVERSITY COLLEGE WINCHESTER
LIBRARY

on corbels ; and the semicircular arch over this is of four
orders, the uppermost of which projects considerably from the
wall.   On either side there are five shafts, the outermost order
having two, which are placed on the front of the jamb and
share one abacus.   These two shafts are worked on the stones

of the jamb—a mode
of construction not very
common in such early
doorways.   The details
resemble those of the
less elaborate doorway
in the other transept, but
some of the foliage on
the capitals here is al-
most   Early   English.
This doorway is ap-
proached by five steps,
and was once covered
by a Renaissance porch.
    In the windows of the
second stage the abacus
of the capitals is con-
tinued as a string from
window to window.   The
two flanking buttresses
have been crowned at
some later period with
gables ending in finials,
and the great gable is
pierced with a Perpen-
dicular window of three
lights, which has three

Ronald P. Jones, Photo.]

DOORWAY, SOUTH TRANSEPT.

transoms in the head, the mullions carried up to the archivolt,
and a dripstone ending in foliage.   The sides of the gable
here do not take an upward turn to meet the corners, and there
are no flanking turrets.   In the end of the aisle the blocked
upper window is pointed, and has a little trefoiled niche above
and to the left of it, and there is no thickening of the masonry
above to necessitate carrying-arches.   The buttresses at the
corner reach to the top of the parapet and have no surmounting
pinnacle.   The small portion of the east side of the aisle which

is not concealed by the Chapter-house and Lady-loft displays in the lower stage a somewhat inexplicable blind arch, carrying an inclined thickening of the masonry that has been afterwards built up to a level, and below the parapet a moulded cornice like that on the north side of the church. This cornice is continued within the Lady-loft, and reappears over the last bay of the choir-aisle.

The Chapter-House.—The south aisle of the choir is concealed by a wing of three storeys, of which the lowest, though exposed to view by the conditions of the site, is of the nature of a crypt, while the second comprises the Chapter-house and vestry, and the third, known as the Lady-loft, is an addition, probably of the fourteenth century. The first two storeys seem to have formed part of a church eariier than Archbishop Roger's,[1] and have been variously ascribed to Archbishops Thurstan (1114–1141)[2] and Thomas of Bayeux (1069–1100).[3] From the east wall of these two storeys an apse is thrown out, upon which rests a square projection from the Lady-loft, too short to be called a chancel. The two westernmost buttresses, up to the string above the crypt, are evidently additions by Archbishop Roger, while the third, which completely encases a three-sided apsidal projection at the corner of the vestry, is of much later date and will be examined presently. Adjoining it is a flat pilaster buttress, apparently original. The crypt has five unglazed windows along the south side, all round-headed and plainly splayed, and, where it joins the transept, there is a large rectangular squint which gives light to a staircase that leads up to the Chapter-house. A pointed doorway, made in later times, cuts into the fourth window from the west. In the second storey there are on this side only four windows, which are spaced without any regard to the position of those below. The two westernmost, which are circular and without tracery—a type of window that is somewhat rare—can hardly be later than the time of Archbishop Roger, and may be earlier : the next two are square and of much later date. Above the windows

---

[1] *I.e.*, they were probably a Southern Chapel of the choir (*vid. inf.*, Ch. III.). It is doubtful whether this earlier choir itself can have had a crypt.

[2] By Sir Gilbert Scott.

[3] By Walbran.

the eaves of the original roofs remain, supported on a corbel-table which is carried round the apsidal chamber at the corner and round the eastern apse. At the south side of the latter the builders have left a narrow recess which extends from the ground nearly to the top of the crypt.

The apse displays in the lower storey a round-headed un-glazed window like those along the south wall, and in the upper storey a small round-headed light at the south side and a larger window in the middle, of the same size as that below, but not so deeply splayed, and with the head rudely trefoiled. On either side of these central windows, a shaft, made in short joints, runs up the apse from base to eaves. The string between the two storeys is carried round these shafts, and their circular bases overhang the plinth and rest on small blocks, while the capitals are square-topped, as in Arch-bishop Roger's work. From the roof of this apse and of the apsidal chamber at the corner, and from the eaves that project along the south wall, it would seem that the whole structure was roofed with stone at a steep inclination. Where its wall joins the transept the stone-work seems to be of the same date on both sides of the corner, so that there may have been an original buttress or wall extending southwards from this point.

The third storey is now the Cathedral library, but was originally the **Lady-chapel**, and was commonly called the Lady-loft. Such a position for a Lady-chapel—at the south side of the choir, and in an upper storey — is extremely unusual.[1] Authorities have differed widely as to its date. Some have assigned it to about 1482 ; but the Lady-loft is clearly mentioned in the Treasurers' Rolls in 1470, and its architecture, which is Decorated rather than Perpendicular, would be in favour of ascribing it to the middle of the previous century, were it not for a certain coarseness of execution which makes a suspension of judgment advisable.[2] To support this additional storey, the two western buttresses were carried up, diminishing both in projection and in width, to within a few feet of the upper string-course. The huge buttress

[1] Lady-chapels are usually found at the extreme east end of the choir, unless that position was wanted for the resting-place of a local saint.

[2] Walbran favoured 1482 ; Sir Gilbert Scott the middle of the fourteenth century.

at the corner was very possibly added later, to counteract a settlement which is evident to anyone so standing as to bring the shafts on the apse in line with the corner of the choir, and which was doubtless due to the weight of the Lady-loft. This buttress is of the same height as the others, but is broader, and has as many as seven stages, the fourth of which is crowned by a truncated hip roof and pierced with a slit to light the apsidal chamber within, from whose sloping top the upper stages spring. Traces of some external means of access to this apsidal chamber from below may be seen at the west side. Except one small lancet adjoining this buttress, the windows of the Lady-loft are square-headed, with mullions branching out into intersecting arches whose cusps spring from the soffit independently of the mouldings—an early feature ; and the dripstones are square labels terminating in foliage, but with the ends not returned. Altogether these are more like the windows of a castle or manor-house than of a church. The four towards the south are of three lights, but the east window has five lights and is set higher in the wall, while its dripstone terminates at one end in a grotesque sitting figure. Various gargoyles project from the string-course, which rises to pass over the east window. The angles of the east end seem to rest upon the very edge of the cornice of the apse, and one wonders how the wall is supported along the chord of the curve. In reality, however, the apse is not so sharply curved internally as externally, and its walls are very thick, so that the square form could be imposed upon the round without much overlapping. The parapet shows the same wide merlons and cruciform piercings which characterize the other Decorated parapets of the church, and it may have been brought forward from the choir-aisle.

The last bay of the latter displays a window like those on the north side, but having foliage on the capitals of the shafts ; and below the parapet runs the cornice continued from the transept, with a curious gargoyle upon it. Part of the base of Archbishop Roger's choir-aisle is visible imbedded between this wall and the apse.

Those parts of the church which were rebuilt after the collapse of the south-east corner of the tower can be best examined from the roof of the Lady-loft, which forms with the roofs of the aisles a level surface of considerable extent.

The East Side of the South Transept has three buttresses, crowned by pinnacles of which the two nearest to the tower are modern. The central buttress is much shallower than the others and has a different termination. The clearstorey displays three well-arched windows of three lights (the innermost window a little smaller than the others) with tracery not unlike that in the south aisle of the nave. The parapet is probably old Decorated work that has been used again, for it has the wide merlons and cruciform piercings characteristic of early battlements, and the Perpendicular pinnacles, it will be noticed, are not in the middle of the merlons. The manner in which the corner of the tower has been reconstructed is extremely interesting. Up the angle formed by choir and transept runs a sort of excrescence of masonry that blossoms out, so to speak, into an extraordinary complication of corbelling near the top, and is itself corbelled away at the bottom. In this excrescence, as elsewhere, old materials have been used again, and in the projecting mass, at the level of both triforium and clearstorey, are the springings of arches curving eastwards and southwards, which suggest that the adjoining walls had at first been intended to be on a more advanced plane, and that the arches of the triforium were to have been round in the transept (where, by the way, they are recessed) as they are in the choir. This angle contains the tower staircase, which is lighted by a little window in the upper corbelling and is reached from the clearstorey gallery of the transept. On this side of the church the parapet walk has to be carried round the corners of the tower on squinches.

The Central Tower. South and East Sides.—The south and east faces are each divided by a central pilaster running up to the top of the parapet, but otherwise the general scheme is not unlike that of the older sides, save that the windows here are set higher in the wall. Each window has two lights, wide and low, with much tracery above them, in which the mullion branches into two sub-arches; and there are dripstones ending in heads. The high weathering on these sides indicates that it was not in the Perpendicular period that the roofs of the church were so unfortunately lowered. At either end of each of these sides a buttress rises to the base of the parapet in three stages, the second of which has on the front a panel with an ogee crocketed hood and is crowned by a gable with a grotesque at each corner, while the

Watson, Ripon, Photo.]

RECONSTRUCTED ANGLE OF THE GREAT TOWER,
(SOUTH TRANSEPT AND CHOIR.)

third is narrower, but is also panelled. Various gargoyles project from the uppermost string, which on the east side is not broken by the central pilaster. As this string is higher than the corbel-table of the older sides, the tower presents a very curious appearance when seen from the south-west or north-east.[1] The battlements and pinnacles were perhaps first added when the south and east sides were rebuilt, but in places they have been much renewed. The stair-turret is surmounted by a hexagonal stone cap, which is pierced with a spire-light and crowned by a finial; and there is also a wooden polygonal bell-cote at the north-west corner of the tower. At the north-east angle the Perpendicular masonry turns the corner and enfolds the Transitional buttresses, where it stops with a jagged edge. This unfinished work has a considerable projection from the Transitional walling, the intention having been, perhaps, to correct externally the obliquity in the ground plan of Roger's tower;[2] it is also corbelled away at the bottom, probably to afford freer passage along the parapet walk and to avoid the necessity of a squinch. Originally the tower had perhaps a low pyramidal roof without a parapet, and then came several successive spires. The last of these, which fell in 1660, is said to have been 120 feet high from the top of the tower, and its disappearance has surely done more than anything else to spoil the external effect of the building.[3]

The South Side of the Choir.—Here the three westernmost bays are Perpendicular and the others Decorated. The westernmost window is smaller than the rest, and is of three lights, with the mullions carried up through the head. The next two windows imitate in curvature their Decorated neighbours, and are of four lights, with the central mullion branching out to form two sub-arches, between which a foliated circle, a feature not common in Perpendicular windows, is introduced

---

[1] See the illustration, p. 2.   [2] *The Builder*, February 4th, 1893.

[3] This last spire must have been erected after all intention of rebuilding the north and west sides of the tower had been given up, and therefore (perhaps) after the dissolution. The three spires are shown upon the seventeenth century communion plate and in several old prints (see the illustration, p. 32). They were wooden and covered with lead, and are represented as octagonal. The two at the west end are shown without parapets at the base, and all three are without those sloping spurs which so often connect an octagonal spire with the corners of the tower.

Ronald P. Jones, Photo.]

FLYING BUTTRESSES, SOUTH SIDE OF CHOIR.

into the head. In the fourth bay the Decorated arch has been filled with Perpendicular tracery, but the fifth and sixth windows remain in their original beauty as on the north side, save that in the easternmost the small circles have been mutilated and have lost their foliation. The two flying buttresses resemble those on the north side, but from the points where they meet the wall two pilasters run up into the parapet, which is flush with them and is crowned by a plain coping, while beneath it is a string, with gargoyles. Except at this end the wall, as in the clearstorey of the nave, is not buttressed, notwithstanding the size of the windows and their nearness together.

The East End.—The rebuilding of the east end of Archbishop Roger's choir was probably the object of an indulgence of 1284 by Archbishop Wickwaine, a brief of 1285 by Pope Celestine V., two indulgences issued in 1288 and 1300 respectively by Archbishops Romanus and Corbridge, and some credentials issued by the latter in 1302 for a collector of funds. And yet it is hard to fix the date of the work with any exactness. It had apparently not begun in 1286, for a mandate of Archbishop Romanus in that year begins *Cancellus Rypon' ruinosus reparetur*; but it may have been completed before the irruption of the Scots in 1318. Two indulgences of Archbishop Melton, one of which is dated 1328, do indeed allude to some "new work" as still unfinished, but this "new work" may have been the repairs necessitated by the violence of the Scots.[1] The east end of the Cathedral, then, recalls that period in our history when Edward I. was wrestling with the Scottish problem, and was also carrying into effect those lessons in representative government which he had learnt from Simon de Montfort.

The well-marked plinth of this east end has been already noticed. Either corner of the choir contains a staircase, and is strengthened by a pair of massive buttresses and crowned by an octagonal turret with a conical stone cap and a finial. These buttresses have a projection of 8 feet, rise to the top of the aisles, and are surmounted by gables with finials, and at the north corner the gables and the coping of the aisle are

---

[1] Dean Waddilove, in his monograph on the Cathedral, mentions that the date 1330 is to be found upon the choir, but he does not say where. Walbran believed the work to have been executed between 1280 and 1297, and is followed by Sir Gilbert Scott.

crocketed. At the south corner the upper part of the turret has been used as a cell. It is lighted by a small slit and has

Ronald P. Jones, Photo.]

THE EAST END.

a wooden floor with a trap in it, from which a ladder once descended to the head of the staircase; and at the west side, in the parapet of the aisle, there is a garderobe seat. It would be interesting to know whether this turret was a prison, or a place of penance, or whether it was occupied by a watchman or sentinel, or, as is not improbable, by one of those recluses who were so often attached to religious communities in the middle ages. The central compartment is flanked by two huge buttresses, which have a projection of 10 feet at the bottom and rise to the base of the gable, or rather a little above it, in two stages only, the lower stage reaching a little above the coping of the aisles, and both stages are crowned by gables with finials.[1] The three compartments of the front are on the same plane. Each aisle shows at the end a window of the same pattern with these in the sides, and that in the south aisle has foliage on the capitals of its shafts and is surmounted by a little window of trefoil form which lights a staircase within, for staircases ascend over these windows in the thickness of the wall and run up the angles of the clearstorey.

The great window in the central compartment is one of the finest examples of Geometrical tracery, if not one of the largest windows, in England. It is over 50 feet high, is 25 feet wide, and has seven lights. Of these the three at either end are comprised under a sub-arch, in the head of which are three cinquefoiled circles, while the central light of the seven is surmounted by an arch, not so high as its neighbours, but impaling upon its acute point a huge circle which fills the head of the window and contains six trefoils radiating from its centre. The arch of this superb window is rather acutely pointed and richly moulded, and has two very slender shafts worked on the stones of either jamb, with foliage on their capitals. Just above the ground below this window there may be observed in the wall one of the many architectural puzzles in which the Cathedral abounds, a half-arch, rising toward the right and filled in with masonry, except at the right side, where is a narrow opening that runs in for a few feet.[2] A

---

[1] The buttresses of this east wall were formerly connected at the bottom by a debased battlemented wall, and the space within was used for sheds, the grooves for whose pent roofs can be seen on the sides of the buttresses.

[2] The arch springs from the buttress (as an excavation in 1900 showed), and may perhaps be a relieving-arch, to take the weight off a weak place in the foundations. Yet it was not intended, apparently, to be filled up. The stones forming the right edge of the hole are coigns, and have mason-marks on their sides. At the back of the hole the masonry appears to be

string-course continued from the sides of the aisles passes below the three windows and round the buttresses, which are further relieved at a little height above it by a set-off. The gable has been entirely rebuilt by Sir Gilbert Scott. It is slightly set back, and displays a lofty window of four lights with geometrical tracery not unlike that in the great window below. On either side of this window there is panelling graduated to suit the triangular space, and the gable is crowned by an elaborate cross and flanked by two pinnacles which resemble those of the flying buttresses but are larger and have foliage at the corners instead of heads. The original Decorated gable was probably very much of this pattern. Its height was indicated by the weathering on the tower, and it seems to have had flanking pinnacles and graduated panelling. It had, however, been lowered in pitch and had been altered also by the insertion of a rather debased Perpendicular window.[1] Whatever may be thought, therefore, of Sir Gilbert Scott's action in rebuilding it, he has surely improved the general effect of the front, and it is well that one of the roofs, at any rate, should have been raised to the original pitch. What is most to be regretted, perhaps, is the removal of all traces, if any there were, of the chantry of the Holy Trinity *supra summum altare*, which was situated, as its name implies, in the roof, behind the old gable.

In Archbishop Roger's day the choir was probably as long as it is now, and Walbran (followed by Sir Gilbert Scott) believed that the aisles at that period were returned across the east end. If so, the clearstorey must have been a bay shorter than at present, with a pent roof projecting from below it on the east side to cover the returned portion of the aisle. The rebuilding of the east end in the Decorated period was the first operation in which limestone was employed, but much of the old gritstone has been used again.

of some antiquity : may it be part of the foundation of the east end of Archbishop Roger's choir ?

[1] There are several prints of the Cathedral, as it was before restoration, in the Ripon Museum.

Watson, Ripon, Photo.]

THE NORTH-WESTERN PORTION OF THE NAVE.

(Junction of **XII**th and **XVI**th Century work.)

CONJECTURAL VIEW OF INTERIOR OF ARCHBISHOP ROGER'S NAVE BY
SIR G. G. SCOTT.

(By the kind permission of the Archæological Institute.)

CHAPTER III.

THE INTERIOR.

The Nave.—On entering through the west doors a per-
spective is disclosed of 133 feet to the end of the Nave, 170
feet to the Rood Screen, and 270 feet to the end of the Choir.
The Early English builders have preserved two bays of Archbishop Roger's nave and have incorporated them into the
west towers,[1] and the two great tower-arches which they have
cut through the Transitional walling are very fine specimens of
the Early English style. Each of the half-pillars that support
them is a cluster of five large engaged shafts separated by very
deep hollows, and upon every shaft there is a large fillet, which
is carried up into the capital and down over the base. The
base consists of two round mouldings separated by a hollow
and fillets, and overhangs the plinth so much as to suggest that

---

[1] This is what was meant by saying in Chapter II. that in each tower
one side is older than the others.

UNIVERSITY COLLEGE WINCHESTER
LIBRARY

the floor just here has been lowered. The capitals and the arches themselves (which are of three orders) are moulded with rounds and hollows very strongly marked, and the hood of the southern arch terminates eastwards in a bunch of foliage.

The interior of the towers is more richly treated than is usual. Over the tower-arch is a small arcade of four members with clustered shafts, and with a string below, while the other three walls are plain up to the windows, each of which is flanked, as on the exterior, by two blind lancets. The arcading thus formed has clustered and banded shafts (not detached), behind which ran a passage, now blocked, and below the sill, and a little distance apart, are two strings, to the lower of which the sills of all the windows save two descend in steps. The windows are not splayed, and those which now look into the aisles are unglazed, and their flanking lancets are of unequal width. All the arches are much moulded and ornamented with the dog-tooth, and the central shaft of each cluster has a fillet. In each corner a detached shaft springs from a round corbel above the lowest string and rises to the impost of the arches, being banded twice on the way; and from its capital another shaft runs up to the ceiling. The doors to the spiral staircases open into little square lobbies which have vaults with groin-ribs springing from corbels.[1] In the north tower is a modern stained window of some merit.

The two bays of Archbishop Roger's work incorporated in the towers, taken together with another Transitional bay at the east end, make it possible to imagine the whole interior of what must have been the most remarkable nave in England. It was unusually broad. From the ground to the first string (about 16 feet) there was plain wall. Above this was a triforium (if it can be so called [2]) of the unusual height of about 28 feet, and there were thus no windows except in the clear-storey, and there only in alternate bays. According to Sir Gilbert Scott the triforium and clearstorey were probably con-

[1] In the interior of these towers the courses run level with those of Arch-bishop Roger's work—a fact which has been taken as indicating that the lowest portion of the towers internally (but not, of course, the tower-arches) may be actually his work. The theory that his west front was flanked by towers or chambers of some kind is not improbable.

[2] A triforium is properly a gallery, open to the church, between the internal and external roofs of the aisles, but here there were no aisles, and the gallery or passage is in the thickness of the wall.

tinued across the west wall. The bays were alternately broad
and narrow, and there is room for five of each sort. The
westernmost bay shows in the triforium stage a round arch
comprising four pointed arches. Of these the two in the
middle are raised above the others on shafts of two stages, in
the upper of which the capital is circular and its moulding is
continued along the tympanum to the *apices* of the two lower
arches. The tympanum is relieved by a sunk quatrefoil in a
serrated circle, and so is the space under either of the two

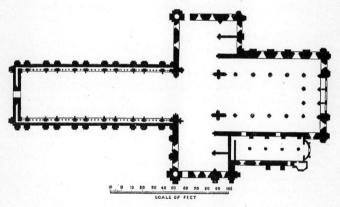

CONJECTURAL PLAN OF ARCHBISHOP ROGER'S CHURCH BY
SIR G. G. SCOTT. See *p.* 16.

(By permission of the Archæological Institute.)

central sub-arches. The passage in this bay has been built up,
and the bay itself shortened, probably when the tower arches
were made.

In the adjoining narrow bay, the comprising arch is pointed,
there are only two sub-arches, and there are no quatrefoils,
except in the tympanum on the north side. Doors have also
been inserted in this bay to communicate with the passages
behind the arcades in the towers.

The shafts throughout are single, and (in the sub-arches)
detached, and the details generally are the same as in all
Archbishop Roger's work. It is worthy of remark that the

tympanum over the sub-arches is flush with the lower part of the wall, and that the comprising arches, with all the walling above them, are a plane in advance. The more natural plan would have been to make the comprising arch flush with the wall below, and to have set back the sub-arches and tympanum. In consequence of Archbishop Roger's arrangement the shafts of the comprising arch stand, not upon the sill of the triforium, but upon corbels, each of which carries two of them and also a roof-shaft[1] which forms with them a cluster.

The clearstorey shows in the broad bay a stilted round arch, pierced, between two small blind lancets, and in the narrow bay three small blind lancets. These arches are not recessed or moulded, and are without hoods, as usual. Their piers, behind which is a passage, are square, and the impost moulding is continued as a string.

The roof-shafts have a curious break in them at the impost-level of the triforium, where a face is carved upon them with a band above it. They are banded also by the impost-moulding of either storey, and by the upper string-course, and end in square-topped capitals a little short of the present roof. Throughout Archbishop Roger's church the roof was probably flat, or slightly coved as at Peterborough. The corbels from which the roof-shafts spring are moulded and finished off with scrolls, and are placed at the level of the string-course, which is undercut; but on either side of the tower-arches the shafts have been shortened to a point above the string, which has been made continuous beneath them, and instead of corbels they have grotesque heads carved upon their ends. Beyond the westernmost roof-shaft there is a further shaft, which at first sight seems to have been the beginning of another bay, but the round moulding which rises from it runs up vertically instead of curving over to form an arch.

The western wall is far more impressive from within the church than from without, and shows the Early English style at its best. The three doorways have stilted segmental arches moulded with rounds, and their hood-moulds are continuous. Their shafts are single and engaged, and in the jambs are holes for the great bars which no doubt held the doors against the Scots in 1318. But if the doorways are

[1] This term will be used wherever the usual term 'vaulting-shaft' is inapplicable.

plainer, the great lancets above are much richer, on this side than on the other. Their arches have more mouldings, their hood-moulds as well as the string-courses are enriched with the nailhead, the dog-tooth is used more profusely, and the piers are clusters of seven engaged shafts instead of five, banded at half their height and having behind them in both tiers passages which formerly communicated with the towers. The glass, by Burlison and Grylls, is worthy of its framing. It was put up to the memory of the late Bishop in 1886. In the lower tier "the earthly type" is represented by the Parable of the Ten Virgins. In the upper tier, in which the various designs represent "the Heavenly type," the Bride is the Church, and Our Lord is seen enthroned and surrounded by choirs of angels.

The yellow gritstone of the older work is contrasted curiously with the white limestone of the Perpendicular nave, and at the junction the later builders have left a jagged edge. Among very late Gothic buildings there are few indeed which are of so good a quality as this nave of Ripon, which, like the late church towers of Somerset, shows that mediæval art took long to die out in regions remote from London. It is, indeed, the architecture of the days of Agincourt rather than of the eve of the English Renaissance. The pillars are characteristic of the Perpendicular style, their section being a square with a semi-circle projecting from each side, and the corners hollowed. Their bases have complex plinths of considerable height and are polygonal, but follow roughly the form of the pillar, and the mouldings, as usual in this style, overhang the plinth. The capitals, with small mouldings and many angles, are of somewhat the same form as the bases. On the westernmost complete pillar of the north arcade are two shields, charged respectively with the arms of Ripon (a horn) and of Pigott of Clotherholme. The arches, instead of being of that depressed form which is so common in late work, are very beautifully proportioned, and their mouldings are bold, numerous and well-cut. There is no triforium ; but a passage, at a slightly lower level than in Archbishop Roger's bays, runs below the great clearstorey windows, which were once, no doubt, gorgeous with stained glass. Their arches are moulded, but the splay is left plain. The roof-shafts, which are in clusters of three and have fillets upon them, spring from semi-octagonal corbels, and where each cluster passes the string-course there is

Ronald P. Jones, Photo.]

THE NAVE, LOOKING WESTWARDS.

an angel holding a shield. A sign of decadence may be
found, perhaps, in the way in which the hood-moulds of the

windows intersect with these shafts. Though the two sides of
the nave are not quite of the same date, they are almost alike,
but for some slight differences in the capitals, the arch-mould-
ings, and the hollows on the pillars; the builders feeling doubtless that any marked variation would mar the general perspec-
tive—a consideration which, of course, could not bind them in
designing the north aisle. The original Perpendicular roof may
have resembled that which now covers the transepts. About
1829 Blore put up an almost flat ceiling of deal. The present
oaken vault, by Sir Gilbert Scott, was copied from that of the
transepts of York Minster, and is adapted to the old roof-shafts,
between which have been added angel corbels of wood. As
the ribs intersect near their springing, they weave a network
over the whole vault, and the carved bosses at the intersections
amount to 107. A passing notice is merited by the pulpit,
which is Jacobean.

East of the five Perpendicular bays remains the second
fragment of the old nave, namely, a portion of a broad bay,
partly encased by the later masonry, and one complete
narrow bay. In the latter the tympanum on both sides is
relieved by a quatrefoil, which here is pierced and not enclosed
in a circle, and the last shaft eastwards (one of those of the
comprising arch) runs to the ground. Affixed to the north
wall is an eighteenth century monument to Hugh Ripley, last
Wakeman and first Mayor of Ripon (d. 1637). The original
monument was destroyed during the Civil War, but the altar-
like erection below the present structure was probably part of it.
The roof-shaft west of this bay, for some unknown reason, ends
considerably short of the roof in a kind of corbel with rude
foliage upon it. In the south wall is a triangular piscina, which,
if it is of Roger's date, is among the oldest piscinæ in the country.

The Saxon Crypt, sometimes called **St. Wilfrid's
Needle.**—From a trap-door in the pavement below the piscina
a flight of twelve steps winds down into a flat-roofed and
descending passage, $2\frac{1}{2}$ feet wide and slightly over 6 feet high,
which, running a few feet northwards and bending at right
angles round the south-west tower pier, extends eastward for
about 10 yards, with a descent of one step near the end, and
terminates in a blank wall. There is a square-headed niche at
the turn and a round-headed niche at the end, both meant,
doubtless, to hold lights. Three feet from the end a round-

headed doorway, 2 feet wide and over 6 feet high, opens northwards, with a descent of two more steps, into a barrel-vaulted chamber, 11 feet 5 inches long from east to west, 7 feet 7 inches wide, and 9 feet 10 inches high. In the north wall of this chamber, and approached by three rude steps, is the celebrated St. Wilfrid's Needle, a round-headed aperture pierced through into a passage that runs behind. This aperture was connected with one of those superstitions that so often flourished before the Reformation in notable centres of religion, and ability to pass through it or 'thread the needle' was regarded

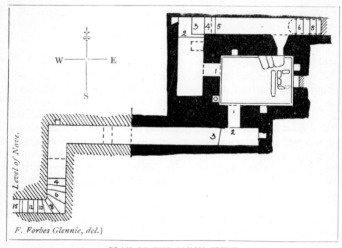

F. Forbes Glennie, del.]

PLAN OF THE SAXON CRYPT.
(From drawings by Mr. W. H. St. John Hope and Mr. T. Wall.)

as a test of female chastity; but it was, of course, in the later middle ages that this superstition arose, and the 'needle' (or rather needle's eye) is evidently only one of the original niches with the back knocked out. Of these niches (which again were doubtless for lights) there are four in the chamber besides the 'needle,'—one in each wall,—and, like the niche at the end of the passage of entrance, they all have semicircular heads each cut in a single stone. That in the west wall has a hole or cup at the bottom, probably to hold oil in which a wick might float, while the others (except the 'needle') have a sort of funnel at the top, doubtless to catch the soot from lamps. In

Watson, Ripon, Photo.]

THE SAXON CRYPT, EAST END OF THE CENTRAL CHAMBER.

(St. Wilfrid's needle on the left.)

the east wall there is also a round-headed recess of larger size, the meaning of which will be discussed later. An excavation made in 1900 has lowered the earthen floor and revealed a set-off running round the chamber,[1] and upon the ground at the east end are traces of a later mediæval altar, namely, a long stone parallel with the east wall and having behind it a small rectangular enclosure bounded by other wrought stones. Some of the latter were only laid bare at the above-mentioned excavation, when, moreover, the enclosure was found to be a pit containing bones, some of which had belonged to a man, others to an ox, others to a bird. These were probably regarded as relics, and may have been buried here at the Reformation for safety,[2] but it is possible that they were placed here at an earlier period, and that this is an instance of a relic-pit. Two other deposits have been found in the crypt in modern times, one behind the niche in the south wall of this chamber, the other behind the niche at the end of the passage of entrance. Most of the bones in these deposits were human, but one had belonged to an ox, another to a bird, another to a sheep, while others could not be identified. These bones again were probably 'relics,' and had almost certainly been built up behind the niches at the Reformation [3] for concealment. From the west end of the chamber another doorway similar to the last opens, with an ascent of one step, into a second chamber, 12 feet long from north to south, 4 feet wide, 9 feet high, and roofed with a semi-vault rising eastwards, in which there has been a square opening, probably for ventilation. At the north end a flight of four steps, lighted doubtless from the square niche in the west wall, ascends eastwards to the passage behind the 'needle.' Of these steps the lowest occupies the whole width of the chamber, while the second, on being cleaned at the time of the excavation above-mentioned, was found to have its upper and western surfaces sunk in the middle and traversed at one end by two parallel raised bands, and to show traces of that yellow enamel-like substance with which, indeed, the whole crypt seems to have been originally overlaid. In roof, width and height the passage at the top of these steps resembles that by which the

---

[1] The earth here has apparently been brought in from outside. Can it have come from some sacred spot abroad? The original floor, if not earthen, may possibly have rested on the set-off.

[2] It has been suggested, however, that they may be relics of a feast buried here to defile the site of the altar. The bones in question are now in the Lady-loft.

[3] With one of the deposits was found a brass bodkin of the type used in the sixteenth century.

crypt was approached, but it is spanned at the entrance by a round arch, and gradually ascends, terminating in a staircase now blocked at the fourth step (or perhaps the fifth, since one seems to have been removed at the bottom), while in the roof may be traced the shape of the long opening (rounded at the western end) through which these stairs once led up into the church. From the point at which they are blocked the distance to the arch that spans the passage is about 18 feet. It will be noticed that the floor of this passage is level with the 'needle,' which on this side, moreover, has been broken through so as to open out like a funnel.

There is little doubt that this crypt is the work of Wilfrid. It strongly resembles another at Hexham in Northumberland, which is almost certainly his since it agrees with a description given by his contemporary Eddius, and (more fully) by Richard, Prior of Hexham in the twelfth century. As, therefore, Wilfrid is known to have built a church in either of these places, and as the crypts remaining resemble each other, and as that at Hexham is almost certainly his, it is natural to conclude that this at Ripon is his also.[1] And the subject has had fresh light thrown upon it as archæology has progressed. It is thought that the Romanizing party which prevailed at the Synod of Whitby affected for its churches the Italian type,[2] one of the characteristics of which was the *Confessio*, an underground chamber for relics [3] situated under the high altar, and surrounded, except toward the church, by a passage reached by steps from the body of the building, whence, moreover, there were generally steps leading up to the floor of the presbytery, and sometimes an incline stretching down to a window that looked into the chamber below. Now the present entrance to this crypt at Ripon is not original. To mention some of the evidences of this, there are in the roof of the passage several tombstones (one at the entrance and two beyond the bend) bearing incised crosses of the thirteenth

[1] It was Walbran, again, who gave these reasons for assigning the crypt to Wilfrid. Before his time it was thought to have been built during the Roman Occupation.

[2] See article by Mr. J. T. Micklethwaite, V.P.S.A., in *Archæol. Journ.*, vol. xxxvii. p. 364.

[3] A *confessio*, it need hardly be said, has nothing to do with a confessional. The word is probably to be explained as meaning the tomb of one who had been a witness or *confessor* of the Faith.

century, and 15 feet west of the doorway into the central chamber there are signs that a cross-wall has been cut through. The only part of the work, then, which is original is that which extends eastwards of this point, and in Saxon times there was probably only one entrance to the crypt, namely by the north passage ; indeed, it seems likely that the formation of an approach from the nave was contemporaneous with the blocking of that passage, and that both alterations were due to the incompatibility of the original disposition of the crypt with the subsequent arrangements of the church above. Now if that original disposition has been indicated correctly, the crypt presented all the more important characteristics of a *confessio*. There is the central chamber with a window looking into it (for this is the probable explanation of the arched recess in the east wall),[1] and there is the surrounding passage, which, however, is interrupted at the south-west corner of the crypt in such a way that it is necessary to pass through the chamber itself.[2] An excavation made in 1891 [3] failed to reveal any traces of a staircase at the east end of the south passage, but as there are many instances in Italy of a *confessio* without a second stair, this failure is of little importance. If, then, this crypt may be assumed to be a *confessio*, there follows a very interesting consequence. The fact that the surrounding passage was entered from the east, that it runs round the west and not the east end of the central chamber, and that the blocked window (if such it be) is in the east wall of the latter, indicates that the nave lay to the east,[4] in other words, that the presbytery was at the west end of the church. Such a position for the high altar is ultra-Roman, was already being discontinued in Wilfrid's day, and had probably never been seen in the north, unless here and at Hexham ; all of which considerations, in the

[1] In making excavations for laying the wind-trunk of the organ the exterior of this wall was laid bare and appeared extremely rough. This, however, does not prove that it had never been meant to be seen. It may have been faced with smooth stones, which, just because they were exposed, attracted attention, and were removed by later masons for use elsewhere.—*Mr. Micklethwaite.*

[2] Among the five known Saxon crypts (all of the *confessio* type) Ripon and Hexham alone show this peculiarity.

[3] See *Proceedings Soc. Antiq.*, 16th June 1892.

[4] In making the above-mentioned excavation in 1891, Mr. Micklethwaite found what was presumably the floor of the body of Wilfrid's church. It was of plaster 3 inches thick, and was 1 foot 7 inches below the floor of the present Cathedral.

light of the known bias and character of Wilfrid, are in favour of the theory above propounded.[1] It is impossible to say with certainty whether Wilfrid's pres- bytery was apsidal or square ; and whether his church had aisles or not.[2]

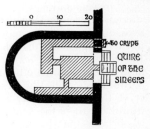

CONJECTURAL PLAN OF THE CRYPT AND PRESBYTERY IN THE TIME OF WILFRID, BY MR. J. T. MICKLETHWAITE, V.P.S.A.

(By permission of the Archæological Institute.)

There remains the question whether this crypt was or was not under the church of the monas- tery. In Leland's description of Ripon,[3] "the Old Abbay of Ripon" is certainly represented as having stood on the site which in Leland's time was occupied by the Lady-kirk, adjacent, that is, to the west side of the street now called St. Mary-gate ;[4] and it has been argued with great ability[5] (on the supposition that "the Old Abbay" means the Saxon Monastery) that this crypt, though almost certainly Wilfrid's, was under a second church outside the monastery wall.[6] It is, however, still possible to suppose that the site in St. Mary-gate may have been that of the domestic

[1] The explanation of the crypt as a *confessio* is due to Mr. Micklethwaite, and is ably set forth, with its consequences, in *Archæol. Journ.*, vol. xxxix. p. 347.

[2] The square termination of the crypt is in favour of a square presbytery ; while his Roman proclivities are perhaps slightly in favour of an apse, and of aisles.

[3] *Surtees Soc.*, vol. lxxiv. p. 83.

[4] It is certainly true that numerous white *tesseræ* of Italian character, such as Wilfrid might have used, have been dug up on this site (*Murray's Cathedrals*, Pt. 1, p. 172, n. 1). They may, however, mark the site of the domestic buildings and not of the church. Or they may be relics of the Roman Occupation.

[5] By Walbran in *Proceedings Archæol. Inst.*, York Vol. 1846 (pub. 1848).

[6] There is an interesting suggestion in *Murray's Cathedrals*, Pt. 1, p. 172, n. 2, that the church of which the crypt formed a part was built not by Wilfrid but by Eadhead, who, as the supplanter of Wilfrid, would prob- ably be excluded from Wilfrid's monastery, but who may, nevertheless, have employed his workmen. The western position of the altar, however, is against placing the work as late as the episcopate of Eadhead.

buildings only, and that the monastery church stood over this crypt; or that "the Old Abbay" means the Scottish Monastery, the site of which was also probably not far from St. Mary-gate and may have been confused by Leland with that afterwards occupied by the Lady-kirk. Nor in any case, perhaps, are the mere statements of Leland a sufficient foundation for the argument that has been constructed upon them. Indeed, an elaborate *confessio* like this would hardly have been made for any church other than that of the monastery.

And if, after all, Wilfrid's monastery church stood above this crypt, there arises a very interesting probability in connection with that part of the south passage which extends 15 feet westward from the doorway opening into the central chamber, namely that it was the original burial-place of Wilfrid himself, whom Bede declares to have been laid *juxta altare ad austrum*.[1]

The position of the crypt suggests the history of the ground plan of the Cathedral. After the destruction of Wilfrid's Church, the site of his nave became that of the choir, and a nave was added westwards. Thus it came about that the crypt is now in the centre of the building. The central line or axis of the church in all stages of its history has probably always passed over this crypt.

The Aisles of the Nave.—As no aisles were contemplated when the west towers were built, the east side of the latter shows, of course, the same external decoration as the other sides. At the back of the surviving portions of the old nave there may be seen at the western end of either aisle one of Archbishop Roger's buttresses, and at the eastern end a roughened surface where another buttress has been removed. The two buttresses that remain have a large set-off near the bottom, and they do not diminish as they ascend; while from their upper portions, which are visible outside the church, it would seem that they rose to the very top of the walls. At a little over 16 feet from the ground there remains upon them a portion of an external string-course, which is not on a level with any of those on the exterior of the transepts. Either aisle opens into the transept with a massive arch resembling those of the north main arcade, and has along the foot of its wall a bench table, from which rise the vaulting-shafts. But though preparation

---

[1] The suggestion is Mr. Micklethwaite's. *Altare* would, of course, mean the high altar in the presbytery above.

had been made for stone vaulting, the roofs were of wood until the last restoration, when Sir Gilbert Scott put up the present stone groining. The effect is good, but would have been better had there been ridge-ribs and bosses.

The South Aisle contains the font, which was probably among the latest additions to the church before the dissolution, and formerly stood at the west end of the nave. This font is

Watson, Ripon, Photo.]

THE TWO FONTS, TWELFTH AND SIXTEENTH CENTURIES.

raised upon two circular steps, and is octagonal and of blue marble, with the various surfaces of base, stem, and bowl slightly hollowed. The sides of the bowl and also of the base bear shields and lozenges alternately, and upon the base the lozenges are richly carved. In a corner hard by stands another and much older font—probably that of Archbishop Roger's church. It is a circular basin, adorned with an arcade of trefoil arches.[1]

Against the wall a little further eastwards is an altar-tomb of great interest. The marble slab at the top has at one end a bas-relief representing a grove, and in it a lion walking away from a man, who kneels in an attitude of supplication with his back to the lion, while between the two figures is a bird flying toward the man. Tradition says that this is the tomb of an Irish prince who brought back from Palestine a lion that had there become attached to him, but a story of this

BAS-RELIEF IN THE SOUTH AISLE OF THE NAVE.
(Reduced from a rubbing.)

kind was popular in mediæval romances,[2] and the tradition, though of some age, is not, perhaps, very probable. It has been well suggested that the sculpture represents deliverance from a lion in answer to prayer; but as it is possibly only part of a larger composition, its full meaning must still be doubtful.[3] The work is rather Flemish in character, and may be assigned to the fourteenth century, with which date the costume of the man agrees. Thus the slab is considerably older than the wall to which it is now affixed, and it is doubtless older than the lower part of the tomb itself, which may be

[1] A third font (modern) formerly stood in the north-west tower.
[2] It is curious that the same story should be told of Roger de Mowbray, founder of Byland Abbey in this same county. (*Murray's Cathedrals.*)
[3] Another suggestion is that the subject has some connection with the history of the Disobedient Prophet.

of the same date as the aisle. There is a black-letter inscription upon the front of the structure, but it is unfortunately quite illegible. An entry in the Chapter Acts [1] indicates that this tomb was used as a money-table in business transactions between the mediæval townsmen.

The windows have their sides moulded, but somewhat clumsily. That above the font contains the only mediæval glass in the Cathedral, a collection of fragments chiefly of the fourteenth century. Most of these were originally in the great window of the choir, where, being in the upper tracery, they had escaped the violence of Sir Thomas Mauleverer's troopers. Among the figures in the medallions are St. Peter, St. Paul, and St. Andrew, and there is a fine shield of the arms of England, with a border or mantling of France, and surmounted by a label of three points azure.[2] The quality of the glass is exceedingly good, and the window, when the sun shines through it, resembles a screen of gems, and puts its neighbours to shame. The fourth window from the west, however, by Clayton & Bell, is of considerable merit. The vaulting-shafts are in clusters of three, and have overhanging bell-shaped bases with polygonal plinths, while upon the capitals are angels bearing shields, one angel to each cluster. The last two shields eastwards are charged respectively with the arms of Archbishop Savage (1501–1507), and with the three stars of St. Wilfrid. Where these shafts break the string-course under the windows they are encircled by a thin band. Upon the eastern fragment of the old nave there remains in this aisle another portion of Archbishop Roger's external string-course, and also (near the last capital of the arcade) some trace of a band of ornament.

The western end of the **North Aisle** is the Consistory Court, and has been used as an ecclesiastical court since 1722, when Ripon was still in the diocese of York. Over the Chancellor's seat is a modern canopy of stained deal, which formerly surmounted the throne in the choir. The stone base of the railings, with its many projecting angles and its band of delicate quatrefoils, is thought to have formed part of the shrine of St. Wilfrid, and, having been found in fragments, was placed here

---

[1] *Surtees Soc.*, vol. lxiv. p. 92.
[2] But for the label, these arms resemble those of John of Eltham (brother of Edward III.), who died without issue in 1334.

F

by Sir Gilbert Scott.   In this aisle the sides of the windows are partially panelled.   The glass is of little interest, save that in the third window from the west, by Burlison & Grylls, and a few seventeenth century fragments.   The vaulting-shafts here are single, and are half-octagons with their sides slightly hollowed, and they again break the string-course, which rises to pass over the doorway.   Of the shields on their angel capitals the three easternmost are charged respectively with the arms of Fountains Abbey [1] (three horse-shoes), with those of Cardinal Archbishop Bainbridge (1508-1514) (supported by *two* angels), and with the stars of St. Wilfrid.   The arch opening into the transept is not so high as in the other aisle, and upon the space above it are portions of a once external string-course and buttress.

The Central Tower.—It is from the interior of the church that the extent of the repairs necessitated by the partial fall of the tower can best be realized, and it is here that the documentary evidence for their dates may best be summed up.   The catastrophe itself is described in an indulgence of 1450 by Archbishop Kemp, but the repairs had not advanced much by 1459, for in that year a testator bequeaths money to this object, "*cum fuerit in operando.*"   It would seem, however, from an indulgence of Archbishop George Neville that the tower had been partially repaired by 1465. After a bequest in 1466 (the last of a series beginning in 1454), it seems to be next mentioned in the Fabric Roll for 1541-2, and the Chapter Acts speak of the work that remained to be done as late as 1545.   The order, therefore, of the larger operations in the Perpendicular period was probably as follows : —First the Canons remodelled the two ruinous sides of the tower and the east side of the south transept (where the work much resembles that in the tower), then they rebuilt the nave,[2] then the western bays on the south side of the choir (as the late character of the work itself would indicate),[3] and lastly they

---

[1] It is pleasant to find in the church several indications of aid received from the other great ecclesiastical foundation in the neighbourhood.

[2] Taken by itself, the coarseness of the work in the tower and transept would suggest that these parts were later, and not earlier, than the nave.   But (not to mention documentary evidence), if they were later, then the Rood Screen must be later also, which can hardly be the case, the stalls against it being dated 1489.

[3] Probably (as Walbran suggested) with money subscribed for the tower, the completion of which was perhaps the less pressing necessity.

were about to remodel the two remaining sides of the tower when they were checked by the dissolution.

Ronald P. Jones, Photo.]
THE WESTERN ARCH OF THE CENTRAL TOWER.

The planning of the Cathedral is remarkably irregular. Not only is the axis of the choir, as in so many churches, inclined

(here toward the north) but the centre of the Rood Screen is
south of the axis of the nave, and the north side of the tower is
not parallel to the south side, the north-west angle being less
than a right angle. This is the only angle which remains in its
original condition, and here the responds of the two adjacent arches stand upon one circular plinth, their own bases
being, however, rectangular, though following in the upper
mouldings the forms of the shafts. The capitals of the latter
are, as usual, square-topped. The respond of the western arch
has a semicircular shaft upon the front, and a smaller shaft at
the west side, where the pier is twice recessed. The arch itself
springs from the level of the top of Archbishop Roger's triforium, is semicircular, and has more orders toward the west
than toward the east, but the mouldings (chiefly rounds) are
lacking in boldness, and the absence of a hood-mould (both
in this arch and the other) is a disadvantage. The other
respond is concealed by a huge Perpendicular casing, which,
obtruding as it does into the arch, is a very conspicuous
object in the view from the west doors. Upon the piers of
this arch toward the nave are some curious brackets, which
probably supported the original rood-beam.[1]

The northern arch springs from a higher level, and is less richly
decorated than the other, and its form is almost segmental.
It has more orders toward the south than toward the north, and
again the mouldings are chiefly rounds. Its western respond
has a shaft on the front, and at the south side another, which
is banded at the springing-level of the western arch and
carried up to that of the northern arch, where it ends in a
three-sided capital, upon which stands another and very short
shaft, complete with base and capital, that carries the rim of
the arch and an angle of masonry that projects from the corner.
The lower portion of this respond is cased by a rectangular
addition (almost as old as the pier itself), which has upon the
front a massive detached shaft with a circular capital, on which
stands a quaint figure of King James I., brought from the screen
of York Minster. To support an image of some kind may,
perhaps, have always been the purpose of this pillar. It has
been suggested that there is a similar projection concealed
behind the casing of the south-western pier.

[1] In the large mediæval churches there was usually an altar at the east
end of the nave.

Over these two arches is a bold cornice, which possibly once supported a ceiling, and the blind storey above shows in each wall two pairs of plain lancets with the impost-moulding continued as a string, and with a passage behind. In the third storey, where again there is a passage, the two windows in each wall have a third arch (also round) between them, and alternating with these three arches are little lancets which have been blocked as far up as the imposts, their shafts having been first removed. A cornice supports the ceiling, and on the west side there are also some rather inexplicable corbels.

The builders of this tower were certainly misguided in employing round arches to support it, at a time when (as the choir shows) pointed arches of considerable size were in common use, and it would seem that the superior strength of the latter form was not yet fully realized. No stronger specimens of that form are to be found, perhaps, than the arches that support the two remaining sides. Their giant piers are clusters of engaged cylindrical shafts with rounded hollows between, and at each remodelled angle of the tower the two adjacent responds are treated as one whole, presenting seven shafts almost on the same plane. The bases, with their complex plinths and overhanging upper mouldings, are over five feet high, and the capitals are polygonal, with small and shallow mouldings, of which the lowest follows the form of the pier. Slightly stilted, richly moulded, and of many orders, these arches are so lofty as to leave no room for a blind storey above. Though the windows here are set higher in the wall, their rear-arches reach down nearly to the Transitional sill-level. Between the two windows in either wall a shaft springs from an angel corbel at the string-course below the sills, and runs up in a kind of groove, and these two shafts, with another which springs from the junction of the two great arches, end short of the present ceiling in semi-octagonal capitals, while on the east wall, and at a lower level, there are more corbels. Indeed, from the various corbels and shafts in this storey it would seem that the level of the ceiling had been altered, possibly more than once, and perhaps that it was destined to be altered again when the remodelling should be complete. The present ceiling, flat and painted with good effect, was put up by Sir Gilbert Scott.

The Transepts.—The length of either transept is 43 feet, and that of both together (including the crossing) is 134 feet, or about the same as the length of the nave. In the transepts and choir the relative proportion of the three storeys or stages to one another, which in the nave was so remarkable, becomes more ordinary, and the change in the level of the triforium passage—due to the heightening of the lowest stage to meet the exigencies of aisles—necessitates long staircases (now blocked) behind the western piers of the tower ; and the same is the case (though in a less degree) with the clearstorey, which in this part of the church is loftier, instead of being shorter, than the triforium. In either transept a bench-table runs along the west wall, and the large lower windows are plainly splayed, but have their sills stepped. The glass in them is bad, except some seventeenth century pieces in the window over the north door. The roof, which is of oak, and Perpendicular, had been concealed in the time of Blore by sham Norman vaulting constructed of *papier maché*. Sir Gilbert Scott re-moved this abomination and exposed the old ceiling, which he repaired and partially renewed. It is almost flat, is raised on wooden figure-corbels, which prevent it from intersecting with the tower arches, and is adorned with judicious colour.

The North Transept, which is 34 feet wide, or 52 feet if the 'aisle' be included, is almost as its builders left it, and is among the most famous examples of the architecture of the age of Henry II. and Thomas à Becket, when the early English style was being developed from the Norman. As the details are the same here as in all Archbishop Roger's work, they need no further description. To take the west and north walls first, the Perpendicular arch opening into the aisle of the nave cuts into two blocked round arches, of which that on the right was a window, while that on the left is backed by the old nave wall ; and in this first bay (which is narrower than the others in both this and the opposite wall) the triforium arches are blocked up, as well as the first lancet in the clearstorey, where there is moreover no window. Each bay shows in the triforium two pointed arches with a pierced quatrefoil between them, and in the clearstorey a stilted round arch, pierced and glazed, between two smaller arches of lancet form, which on the north wall are very curiously barred across at the impost level, the *abaci* of two shafts being formed by one slab.

The east wall is much more richly treated, and harmonizes in design with the choir. It might perhaps be more proper to

Ronald P. Jones, Photo.]

THE NORTH TRANSEPT.

describe the aisles of these transepts as a series of eastern chapels. Their floor is raised two steps above the body of the transept, from which they were evidently once railed off, and in either transept the two outer bays are walled off from that nearest to the tower. At any rate the arches here have the appearance of independent units rather than of a continuous arcade. Separated by roof-shafts of unusual bulk, their responds consist each of three engaged shafts with a fourth to carry the aisle-vault ; and the bases, rectangular but with the upper mouldings following the pillar, are united with those of the roof-shafts, while the capitals as usual are square-topped. The actual arches are of two orders, each of which has the edge-roll, while under the soffit, which is flat, is another roll between two mouldings that are hook-shaped in section. The arch nearest to the tower has given way slightly and has been blocked up, apparently not very long after it was built, for in the blocking wall is an acutely-pointed and thrice-recessed doorway of decidedly early character, and the material throughout is gritstone. The wooden doors are probably Perpendicular work.

Adjoining this doorway is a Perpendicular stone pulpit, which has a base but no stem, and is ascended by means of three steps only. It has five sides, and is covered with rich panelling, but the top has apparently been taken off. This may not indeed be its original position,[1] yet it was a mediæval custom to deliver the sermon just as the procession was about to enter the choir, and this pulpit is most conveniently placed for such a purpose. If this is not its original position, it may perhaps be identified with a nave pulpit mentioned in the Chapter Acts.

On this east side the triforium shows in each bay a semicircular arch comprising two pierced lancets and flanked by two blind lancets, with a quatrefoil pierced through the tympanum under the comprising arch, an arrangement that is the germ of tracery. Here there is no passage in the thickness of the wall, as there was an open gallery over the aisle until the external roof was lowered and the back of the arches blocked.

In the clearstorey the shafts of the round arch in each bay are doubled, each couple sharing a common plinth and capital,

[1] It may have been put here at the time of the building of the present nave, than which it is perhaps slightly earlier.

from which latter springs a tiny shaft that carries the edge-roll of the arch ; and the lancet arches also, where they adjoin the solid piers between the bays, have a shaft in the jamb. On all three walls the shafts in this storey stand on a kind of kerb or parapet, which is interrupted in the middle of each bay, and the stilt of the round arch is treated almost like a classical entablature, and has a moulding or cornice above it, while the uppermost part of the wall is thickened, thereby necessitating over each bay a comprising arch, which on the north wall is round, but on the other walls follows the shape of the three sub-arches, and forms a kind of upper order to them.

The roof-shafts, which do not break the string-courses, spring from very various levels : on the east side from the ground, and on the north side from the unusually high level of the second string, while on the west side one cluster rises from the first string and the other from above the second string (having perhaps been shortened in the last case to make way for the Perpendicular arch beneath). On the east and west walls these shafts are of a thickness which, besides being out of proportion to the other parts of the architecture, is structurally unnecessary, for they do not directly support the roof at all, but end at the top of the triforium in triple capitals, of which the central member is square and the others round. Upon each of these capitals, stand three detached and much thinner shafts—namely, that which really carried the roof-beams, and those (adjacent to it) of the arches that carry the above-mentioned thickening of the wall. Thus is afforded a striking instance of the tendency, so often exemplified in Archbishop Roger's work, to use two shafts, one on the top of the other, instead of prolonging one—a tendency which marks the organic development of the style as still incomplete. On the north wall the three shafts in each cluster are carried up from their corbel to the top in one piece, unbroken save by a band at the impost level of the triforium and another at the third string, and they seem detached throughout their height both from the wall and from each other. At each corner of the transept the thickening of the wall over the clearstorey arcade is carried by a shaft which rises from the bench-table or the ground.

The roof is entirely modern, and the shields on its corbels bear the arms of the chief promoters of the last restoration.

Against the north wall is a fifteenth century altar-tomb,

covered with inferior panelling and shields of arms, and surmounted by the figures of Sir Thomas and Lady (Eleanor)
Markenfield; and adjoining this tomb (which formerly stood
within the aisle) is the lid of a thirteenth century stone coffin
on the floor. In the aisle stands another altar-tomb, which has
the sides panelled and adorned with shields of arms and bears
the figure of an earlier Sir Thomas Markenfield, clad in armour
of the period between Poitiers and Agincourt, and wearing a
very curious collar of park palings with a stag couchant in front,
possibly (as has been suggested) a badge of adherence to the
party of Lancaster. The figure of Lady Markenfield has,
unfortunately, been destroyed.[1]

The aisle is often called the Markenfield Chapel, and doubtless contained the Markenfield family chantry, which seems to
have become afterwards merged in another foundation.[2] The
two bays were apparently once walled off from each other,
the dividing wall having perhaps been removed to make way
for this Markenfield tomb. At any rate, between the bays of
the vaulting there is a plain cross-arch of remarkable thickness, whose eastern respond is cut off above the tomb, as are
also the two adjacent vaulting-shafts, which have had heads
carved upon their ends. The south wall is probably original,
since (to mention one reason) part of the string-course upon
it is worked on the same stone with the vaulting-shaft. The
lower parts of the walls display traces of a design in red
representing round arches interlaced. In the north wall there
is a square aumbry, and in the south wall a large piscina,
with trefoil head and projecting basin. If this piscina is
original, it is a very fine specimen for so early a date. A huge
eighteenth century monument to Sir Edward Blacket of Newby
almost covers the southernmost window, but the remaining
two contain glass of some merit, which in that facing east
commemorates the recovery from fever of King Edward VII.,
then Prince of Wales. The vaulting springs from single
cylindrical shafts, which rise from the ground and do not

---

[1] The Markenfields were one of the principal families in the neighbourhood from the fourteenth century onwards, until in the reign of Elizabeth
they ruined themselves by taking part in the Rising in the North. Their
ancient moated Manor-house, in which both the knights sculptured on
these altar tombs must have lived, is still standing, about three miles from
Ripon, towards Harrogate.

[2] This aisle was also the site of the chantry of St. Andrew.

interrupt the string-course. Their bases have three-sided plinths, and their capitals are enriched with stiff foliage and are three-sided above.

The vaulting, which is apparently original, deserves especial notice. Its bays are square, and the groin-ribs consist each of three round mouldings, of which the most prominent is 'keeled';[1] but what is most remarkable is that there are also

Watson, Ripon, Photo.]

VAULT OF THE NORTH TRANSEPT AISLE, TWELFTH CENTURY.

ridge-ribs, which are not usually found before the thirteenth century, and it has been suggested [2] that this is the earliest instance of their employment. There are also wall-ribs, and these and the ridge-ribs are much thinner than the groin-ribs, and consist of a single roll only.

The South Transept is narrower than the other by a yard, its width being 49 feet to the aisle wall (which, it should

---

[1] In these pages this term is used to describe round mouldings which are brought to an edge without actually having a fillet upon them.
[2] By Mr. Francis Bond.

be noticed, has not been rebuilt).   Without the aisle the
width is only 30 feet, but this is partly due to the Perpendicular
alterations.   The end and west side of this transept, which
remain more or less as they were in Archbishop Roger's day,
resemble the corresponding walls of the other, yet with the
following differences.   The roof-shafts on the west side are
thinner here than there, and are carried up to the required
height in one piece, unbroken save by the string-courses.

In connection with the attachment of shafts of any considerable height to wall-surfaces in Archbishop Roger's work, it will
be observed that though the shafts (according to the general
practice of masonry) are usually made in short joints built in
at the back, yet (as here) their jointing sometimes does not
harmonize with the coursing of the wall ; again (as in the old
nave and north transept) the shafts of a cluster are sometimes
not worked all on the same stones.

To return to the differences of this transept from the other,
the roof-shafts over the inserted Perpendicular arch (which
here obtrudes into the triforium) descend no lower than the
sill of the clearstorey.   Again, the thickening of the walls at
the top is supported in the south-west angle not by one shaft
but by two, one of which stands on a projecting strip of
masonry that runs up the angle to the triforium.   The design
of the eighteenth century monument against the south wall,
to Mr. Weddell of Newby, is taken from that of the choragic
monument of Lysicrates at Athens.

On the east side, which has been entirely remodelled in the
Perpendicular period, the bay next to the tower displays from
the ground to the triforium a plain surface broken only by a
pointed doorway surmounted by three cinquefoiled niches with
ogee crocketed hoods.   The doorway retains its original doors
with an ornamental iron scutcheon over the keyhole.   In their
great strength, and in their treatment generally, the two arches
opening into the aisle resemble the Perpendicular arches of
the central tower.   The triforium stage is exceedingly poor,
and shows traces of more or less modern disfigurement.   Each
bay contains a single arch which does not occupy the whole
space, and which is surmounted by a hood-mould and divided
into two sub-arches, but without cusps.   Here again the arches
were once pierced through to a gallery over the aisle, as the
exterior of the wall plainly shows ; and this seems to indicate

either that the external roof had not been lowered when these Perpendicular repairs took place, or that possibly the two lower storeys of Archbishop Roger's wall were left standing, and have been, not rebuilt, but cased. The appearance of the wall externally suggests that these arches may have once been round, and the unusual bulk of the two aisle-arches seems further to support the theory of a 'casing.' In the clearstorey the windows have hood-moulds, but otherwise are treated much as in the nave. The southernmost contains a fragment of old glass, bearing the words ' Jhesu mercy.' Along the sill of the passage may be seen the stumps of uprights which may perhaps have supported a rail. The roof-shafts are clustered and extremely thick, and appear the more awkward in that the wall and the shafts with it are set back at the base of the triforium. In this transept the ceiling is old, and among the heraldic devices carved upon it are those of the church itself, St. Wilfrid, the See of York, the Pigotts, the Nortons, and Fountains Abbey.

The aisle, the walls of which have not been rebuilt, and which has a chequered pavement of uncertain date, was for some centuries the burial-place of the owners of Studley Royal, and is often called the Mallory Chapel. A curious recess in the south wall is concealed by the monument of John Aislabie of Studley, Chancellor of the Exchequer at the time of the South Sea Bubble, and against the north wall is a monument to that Sir John Mallory of Studley who defended Skipton Castle for Charles I., and delivered Ripon from Sir Thomas Mauleverer. There is a square aumbry to the right of this monument, and in the next bay another, divided by a stone shelf and having modern doors with ornamental iron-work. The northern bay is almost wholly occupied by a stone staircase leading up to two doors, one of which opens on the left into a chamber now containing the bellows of the organ, while the other opens into the Lady-loft or Library. Over the latter door and over the Mallory monument will be observed traces of two original windows, which, before the erection of the Lady-loft, admitted doubtless whatever light was not blocked out by the old roof of the Chapter-house. On this wall hangs a royal escutcheon bearing the motto of James I. The vaulting is Perpendicular, but two of the original supports remain on the east side. The shaft in the south-east corner resembles

those in the Markenfield Chapel, save that its capital has no
foliage ; but between the two bays, instead of two shafts flanking the respond of a thick cross-arch, there is a cluster of
three detached shafts, banded at the string-course, and sharing
a common capital with a semi-octagonal top.   It would seem,
therefore, that the two bays here were never walled off from
one another.[1]   At the north-east corner the vaulting springs
from a Perpendicular corbel.   Its moulded ribs are exceedingly
ponderous, and one of them, not having room to descend
upon the pillar, is finished off with a head.   The present
Library staircase was put up by Sir Gilbert Scott in place of an
older flight attached to the north wall, and upon the latter
may be seen (behind the stairs) traces of mural paintings in
red and green, representing the Adoration of the Magi and
other subjects.   The archaic character of these paintings indicates the age of the wall, which, nevertheless (unlike the corresponding wall in the Markenfield Chapel), seems to have been
an afterthought, since it differs from the other walls in the
coursing of the stone and in the pattern of the string-course,
and, moreover, at its northern end there is a 'straight joint,'
visible in the choir-aisle.

The Rood Screen, according to Sir Gilbert Scott, is of a
date a few years earlier than 1494, but, if so, it has taken the
place of another, which is mentioned in the Fabric Rolls as
early as 1408.[2]   The general design is that of an arched doorway with four large niches on either side, and a tier of twenty-
four small niches over all.   The doorway, which retains its
original panelled doors, has three shafts in either jamb, and is
surmounted by a crocketed ogee hood, under which is a
sculpture representing the First Person of the Trinity with
attendant angels.   A figure of the Saviour evidently once
rested, as Walbran noticed, upon the knees of the central
Figure ; above whose head or shoulder, moreover, there was
doubtless once a representation of the Holy Dove.   The niches
again have crocketed ogee hoods, and in the lower tier

---

[1] In spite of Sir G. Scott's conjectural plan. (See p. 67.)
[2] It is possible that the screen there mentioned may be the present structure, or may have been incorporated into it.   In 1408 the accident to the
tower had not yet occurred, and the piers that now flank the screen had
therefore not yet been built.   There is a not very credible story that the
present screen came from Fountains Abbey.

contain pedestals bearing shields charged with the arms of the Pigotts and other benefactors, while the sill of the last at either end of this tier is considerably raised, and the space below panelled. The niches contain ribbed vaults, and are cinquefoil, with feathered cusping, and their hoods are prolonged so as to divide the members of the upper tier into pairs; while from the sides of these hoods, from the buttresses,

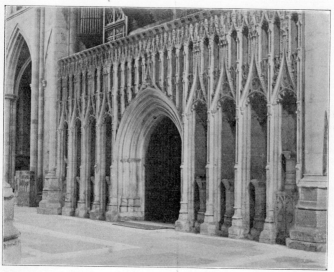

Ronald P. Jones, Photo.]

THE ROOD SCREEN.

and from the curve of the doorway, thin strips of stone, adorned with knobs that distinctly add to the effect, are carried up to the cornice, along which runs a row of shields bearing traces of colour. In the lower part of the screen the spaces between the strips and under the hoods are filled with tracery. The screen is 12 feet thick, and in the passage through it are two doors, that on the right opening into a winding staircase to the loft above, and that on the left into a deep pit, which once communicated, it is thought, with the north passage of the Saxon crypt.

The Choir.—The choir extends 92 feet eastward from the screen. Its width is 33 feet between the columns, or 68 feet if the aisles be included. A notable peculiarity in it is, that after the lowering of the aisle-roofs externally, the triforium was glazed, so that there are two tiers of windows above the main arches.[1] Many styles meet here. The first three bays on the north side are Archbishop Roger's work, while the three opposite are Perpendicular, and lastly, the three easternmost bays on either side are chiefly Decorated.

To begin with the north side. The arch in the first bay has been built up, probably to strengthen the tower, and by the twelfth-century builders themselves, for the abacus-moulding of the capital is continued across the blocking wall. In the latter the fifteenth-century builders have made a small pointed door-way, which is now blocked but apparently once gave access from the top of the screen to a staircase in the north aisle. This and the two next bays bear in all three stages a general resemblance to the east side of the north transept. The columns, however, are clusters of eight cylindrical shafts, and stand upon circular plinths, the base proper follow-ing, of course, the form of the pillar. The capitals, as usual, are compound and composed of plain inverted bells, and have square tops with the abacus hollowed and grooved. The arches differ from those in the transept only in that the large moulding under the soffit is 'keeled,' and that the mouldings which flank it are simple ridges. In the triforium the cusps visible in the glazed sub-arches belong to some tracery which has been applied to the back at a later period.

The treatment of the vaulting-shafts is very remarkable ; indeed, nothing is more instructive than the variety shown in the treatment of this feature throughout Archbishop Roger's church, the different parts of which are suggestive of nothing so much as of a series of architectural experiments. Here, upon the capital of each column, rests a sort of compound rectangular plinth, from which project three corbels, hollowed underneath and having little blocks beneath their overhanging edge. From this plinth and corbels springs a cluster of no

[1] This peculiarity is found at some other places—*e.g.*, St. Cross, Win-chester.

Ronald P. Jones, Photo.]

THE GREAT EAST WINDOW.

G

BAY OF ARCHBISHOP ROGER'S
CHOIR (WITHOUT THE VAULTING).

(From a drawing by Sir G. G. Scott, by
permission of the Archæological Institute.)

less than five shafts, which, by their united width, conceal the springing of the upper order of the main arches. They are banded at the string-course below the triforium, and end at the sill of the clearstorey in a compound capital, of which the three central members are square, and the others round. Upon this capital, apparently, stand the two adjoining shafts that carry the thickening of the wall above the clearstorey, and here (but hidden by the vaulting) stands also the original roof-shaft, and these three are 'detached.' Thus the arrangement is in principle similar to that adopted in the north transept, while at the same time the clustered shafts are even more disproportionate here than there to the slight burden they have to carry; indeed the effect is that of five shafts diminishing to one. The vaulting hides a feature which is not found in the transept, namely, a little lancet arch whose apex comes exactly behind the roof-shaft in each bay.

Though the three eastern bays (still on the north side) are chiefly Decorated, portions of Archbishop Roger's work have been retained or used again. Thus the fourth column from the west is his, and perhaps the fifth up to the abacus, which is convex and of limestone. The respond against the east wall is of his pattern, but it has not the circular plinth, and the capital is of limestone, has the abacus moulded with rounds upon the edge, and is covered with delicate foliage in the Decorated manner. In these arches the lower order has exactly the same mouldings as in the western bays, and is of gritstone, while the upper order is of limestone, and has fillets upon the larger mouldings. It would seem, therefore, that the later builders have used the original archivolts again, and have merely added another order or orders over it. The plane of the wall above, indeed, is brought forward to the face of Archbishop Roger's vaulting-shafts: yet without being really thickened, since it is set back from his wall on the exterior. At the junction of the old vaulting-shafts with the additional order of the first Decorated arch the later builders have carved a group of grotesque faces. In each bay of the Decorated triforium there is a round arch filled with tracery consisting of three round-headed and trefoil lights with two circles enclosing trefoils above them; and on either side of this arch (but on one three only, in the first of the

Watson, Ripon, Photo.]

DECORATED CAPITAL IN CHOIR.

side bays) is a sunk lancet panel enclosing a pointed arch impaling a trefoil. The clearstorey has a second plane of tracery, a feature not very common in England. The vaulting-shafts are in clusters of three and are filleted, and the string-course below the triforium is not carried round them. Each cluster springs from a semicircular corbel resting on a head, and has its capitals enriched with foliage. The last pendentive of the vaulting rests on a single shaft springing directly from a head-corbel. The string-courses are not of the same pattern with those on the older bays.

Watson, Ripon, Photo.]

THE NORTH SIDE OF THE CHOIR.

(Junction of Transitional and Decorated work.)

On the south side the westernmost Perpendicular bay, up to the triforium, is solid and covered with cinquefoil panelling. In the next two bays the mouldings of the arch, among which a broad hollow is conspicuous, are continued down the column,

and there is no capital—a sign of decadence more common
in the Flamboyant work of the Continent than here. There
is, however, a debased half-capital on the east side of the
last Perpendicular column, and on the west side of it are three
small heads at the impost-level. These columns are lozenge-
shaped in section, wider from north to south than from east to
west, and though the mouldings end before they reach the
bottom of the column, there is no proper base. Each
column has a shaft at the front and another at the back,
the former carrying the rim of the arch and having a stilted
polygonal base but no capital, while the latter has capital as
well as base (both polygonal), and helps to carry the aisle-vault.
The spandrels of these arches are filled with panelling, in
which are several shields (one bearing the arms of Pigott).
The triforium again shows in each bay a round arch ; indeed,
no better example than this choir could be found of the
truth that the form of the arch is not a safe guide to
the date of a building, but was often dictated by convenience ;
for here in the triforium are round arches, of which some
belong to the twelfth, others to the thirteenth, and others
to the sixteenth century. The fact that the distance between
the string-courses was already settled by the Transitional
bays, compelled the later builders to make their arches
round, as a pointed arch of the requisite width would
have been too tall. Here the round arch, which is again
flanked by two panels, comprises three cinquefoil lights, and
the mullions are carried up through the head. The panels
are pointed and divided each into two cinquefoil divisions.
The Perpendicular clearstorey windows have their rims
moulded, but are not splayed. The vaulting-shafts resemble
those in the Decorated bays, but their corbels are polygonal
and have the sides slightly hollowed, and the abacus of
the capital is a half-lozenge. The string-courses have not
been made to match either the Transitional or the Decorated.
The whole of this Perpendicular work is of very late character,
and justifies the belief that it was the last important alteration
in the fabric before the dissolution. Moreover, where it
meets the tower there seems to be a 'straight joint,' which
indicates that these bays are at any rate later than the tower
piers.

East of the Perpendicular pillars the next column is Archbishop Roger's, and perhaps the next also, with the exception of its capital, which has two rings upon the necking, with the rectangular top imposed directly upon them and chamfered beneath, while the abacus (which is of limestone) is convex.[1] The respond against the east wall is again of the old pattern, but without the circular plinth, and its capital resembles that just described.   In the westernmost of these southern Decorated bays three styles meet.   The lower order of the arch seems again to be Transitional work, while in the triforium and clear-storey Decorated arches have been filled with Perpendicular tracery.   In the two remaining bays the main arches are entirely Decorated, the lower order being of limestone and the large moulding under the soffit having a fillet.   Over the last two complete columns there is a little foliage, and of the corbels of the vaulting-shafts one is enriched with foliage while the other consists of a head between two embracing figures.   There is foliage upon the capitals of these vaulting-shafts, and upon the capital and base of that which supports the last pendentive of the vaulting.   With the exceptions mentioned, these bays resemble those opposite.

It has been remarked that the choir was probably as long in the twelfth century as it is now.   The point is indeed proved if (as there seems no reason to doubt) the last complete column on either side is original and occupies its original position ; but a further indication is to be found in the fact that the fragment of the original south wall, the end of which is visible on the exterior between the south aisle and the apse, extends well into the last bay of the present choir.[2]

The huge east window, which is not splayed, has a deep rear-vault bounded by a massive rib, whose outer edge rests on slender engaged shafts with foliage on their capitals, while the inner edge ends in bunches of foliage.   Between this rib and the tracery is another rib springing on the north side from a bunch of foliage and on the south from a grotesque corbel.   The inner arch has slender shafts, and so has the moulding next to the tracery, but in the latter case the capitals are plain.[3]   Few acts of

[1] This column and that opposite to it on the north side have been regarded as entirely Decorated imitations of Archbishop Roger's columns, but surely without sufficient reason.

[2] See also the account of the East End in Chapter II., pp. 60-63.

[3] Two holes have been drilled through the rear-vault from the attic above, but for what purpose it is hard to say.

vandalism are more to be regretted, probably, than the destruction in 1643 of the magnificent fourteenth century glass which once occupied this window.

The present very poor glass, by Wailes of Newcastle, commemorates the revival of the see of Ripon in 1863.

Over the window may be seen the mark of one of the earlier roofs. The choir is thought to have received a groined vault of oak after the rebuilding of the east end, but this vault was probably renewed more than once, especially after the accident to the tower about 1450, and the fall of the spire in 1660. Sir Gilbert Scott found a vault of lath and plaster (probably the work of Blore) for which he substituted the present roof, a groined wooden vault, admirable in its lofty pitch and judicious colouring. Its chief feature, however, is the splendid bosses along the ridge, which are survivals from either the Decorated or a subsequent Perpendicular vault. In some of these bosses the figures are five feet long.

A Bishop and a King.

The Expulsion from Paradise.

Watson, Ripon, Photo.]

BOSSES FROM THE CHOIR-VAULT.

From west to east the subjects are as follows : (1) A head ; (2) an angel, with foliage ; (3) a head ; (4) a man conducting a woman to a church door ; (5) a bishop in benediction ; (6) a king enthroned ; (7) a bishop enthroned ; (8) a king and a bishop enthroned together ; (9) the Crucifixion (modern) ; (10) the Annunciation ; (11) the expulsion from Paradise ; (12) ? the good Samaritan ; (13) a head.

There are also good foliage bosses against the walls between

the pendentives. The westernmost pendentive on either side
rests on a Perpendicular corbel carved with delicate foliage.

The general arrangements of the presbytery have been much
changed since the middle ages. The altar then stood against
a screen one bay in advance of its present position, and
the iron hooks upon the second complete column from the
east end on either side held, it is supposed, the Lenten Veil.
Before the last restoration the altar stood, as now, against the
east wall (on a single step, however), but the Sanctuary still
extended two bays westward and was three steps above the rest
of the choir, which was all on one level.   Since then the floor
has been raised one step at the east end of the stalls, and the
steps to the Sanctuary have been diminished by one, while there
are now two steps to the altar, and the Sanctuary and the raised
portion of the choir have received an inlaid marble pavement.
The reredos, an arcading of slender arches each enclosing
a trefoiled arch impaling a trefoil, is a restoration of the original
Decorated work.   The latter had been covered by a painted
screen of wood—possibly of late mediæval workmanship—
and this again by a huge oil-painting of the time of Charles II.
Both were removed to make way for a high reredos by
Blore, which in its turn was taken down by Sir Gilbert Scott.[1]
On the pavement south of the altar is a piscina, which (if this
be its original position) must have belonged to a chapel or
chantry behind the high altar—possibly the chantry of the
Holy Trinity *subtus altare*.[2] From its position it would seem
that in those days the floor here was considerably lower than it
is now.

The Sedilia.—The last bay on the south side is now
occupied by three sedilia and a piscina, which form one block.
As might be expected from the mediæval position of the
altar, they once stood in the second bay from the east, and
they were not removed to their present position until the last
restoration.   Sir Gilbert Scott considered them late Decorated work, but they have rather the appearance of late
Perpendicular.   Over each seat is an ogee canopy, cinque-

[1] It appears from the Fabric Rolls that a new high altar was begun in 1522.
The work seems to have lasted four years, and apparently included a carved
wooden reredos.

[2] *Subtus altare* suggests a crypt, but there seems to have been no crypt
under the choir.   Perhaps the *altare* meant may have stood over the
Saxon or the Norman crypt.

Ronald P. Jones, Photo.]

THE SEDILIA.

foil, crocketed, and surmounted by a huge finial. These canopies rest on square pillars, the sides of which are adorned with a sort of 'four-leaved flowers,' while the capitals are encircled with foliage in which are animals and monsters. Each pillar is surmounted by a pinnacle, and behind each canopy rises a crocketed gable, again crowned by a huge finial. The gables, the pinnacles, and the tops of the canopies are the work of Sir Gilbert Scott, who found the sedilia in a mutilated condition. Below the seats and the piscina runs a chamfer with 'four-leaved flowers' along it, and below this are panels enclosing trefoils containing faces. But the most curious feature of these sedilia is not perceived until a glance is given beneath the canopies. The carved ends of the cusps are in reality the heads of extraordinary grotesques whose bodies are curled up against the under surface of the arch. Some of these figures, in addition to their proper physiognomy, have faces carved on the crowns of their heads. The piscina, which has been converted into a credence table, has another ogee canopy, and is backed by a wall, along the top of which runs a band of foliage that is continued round the top of a square pillar at the end of the block.

The fine oak chairs in the Sanctuary are of modern construction but of old material, while the rails, lectern and pulpit are all modern.[1]

In the four easternmost bays the choir is separated from its aisles (except where the sedilia already block one arch) by elaborate oak screens of various designs, in the upper part of which the tracery is largely pendant—an arrangement characteristic of Yorkshire. These screens have been restored, but contain much of the old work, most of which is probably of the same date with the stalls.[2] Until the last restoration they were surmounted by seventeenth century galleries in the so-called Jacobean style.

The Stalls—thirteen on either side and eight returned

[1] Mention may be here made of the Communion plate, some of which is as old as 1676 and has upon it representations of the church, very incorrect but showing the spires ; also of the mace which is now borne before the Dean, and which has been assigned to the fifteenth century and may possibly have been once borne before the Wakeman. Upon the top has been engraved an *Agnus Dei*, the cognizance of the church.

[2] A piece of woodwork, however, which was in the north aisle at the time of the last restoration, is said to have borne the date 1397.

Ronald P. Jones, Photo.]

CHOIR STALLS, FIFTEENTH CENTURY.

against the Rood Screen—are exquisite specimens of fifteenth century woodwork. They are surmounted by lofty canopies of

elaborate tabernacle-work supported on slender shafts and
rising into a forest of crocketed spirelets and pinnacles. There
are ribbed vaults under the canopies, and upon the pendants
in front are hovering angels. The canopies on the south side
were wrecked by the fall of the spire in 1660, and those over
the eight easternmost stalls were then reconstructed in the
'Jacobean' style with a gallery above, while of the canopies

Jonah emerging from the whale.   Pelican eeding her young.
Watson, Ripon, Photo.]

MISERERES, FIFTEENTH CENTURY.

now over the other nine, eight are said to have been brought
across from the eastern end of the north range, where more
Jacobean canopies were erected in their place. Sir Gilbert
Scott removed all this seventeenth century work and set up
reproductions of the fifteenth century design. Thus the eight
easternmost canopies on either side are modern. The misereres
and arms of the stalls are exquisitely carved.

The subjects upon the former are as follows, beginning from the archway
in the screen :—

North side :—(1) (CANON IN RESIDENCE) lion attacked by dogs ; (2)

dragon attacked by dogs ; (3) angel with shield ; (4) dragon and birds ; (5) hart's-tongue ferns ; (6) conventional flowers ; (7) ape attacked by lion ; (8) vine ; (9) birds pecking fruit ; (10) antelopes ; (11) fox preaching to goose and cock ; (12) fox running off with geese ; (13) fox caught by dogs ; (14) dragons fighting ; (15) fruit and flowers issuing from inverted head ; (16) man holding club with oak leaves and·acorns ; (17) (MAYOR'S STALL) griffin catching rabbit.

South side :—(1) (DEAN) angel with book ; (2) angel with shield bearing date 1489 ; (3) lion *versus* griffin ; (4) griffin devouring human leg ; (5) owl ; (6) mermaid with mirror and hairbrush ; (7) two pigs dancing to bagpipe played by a third ; (8) Jonah thrown to the whale ; (9) man wheeling another who holds a reed and a bag ; (10) fox caught carrying off goose by dog and by woman with distaff ; (11) winged animal ; (12) hart, gorged and chained ; (13) pelican feeding young ; (14) Jonah emerging from the whale ; (15) Samson carrying the gates ; (16) head (modern)[1] ; (17) (BISHOP'S THRONE) Caleb and Joshua carrying the grapes and watched by Anakim.

Most of these misereres have exquisite conventional flowers (especially roses) cut upon them in addition to the figure-subjects. The desks in front of the stalls have

Rev. E. H. Swann, Photo.]

DESK-END OF MAYOR'S STALL.

rich finials, and their panelled fronts form the backs of a lower tier of seats, the arms of which are supported each on a square shaft set diamondwise. In front of these

---

[1] The old miserere was probably removed when the Throne was made to comprise two stalls. (*See* p. 111.)

lower seats the desks again have carved finials and panelled fronts, and on those parallel with the Rood Screen the tracery is distinctly Flamboyant.   The finial before the stall

Rev. J. Beanland, Photo.]

FINIAL IN FRONT OF THE BISHOP'S THRONE.

of the Canon in Residence has a griffin attached to it, and that in front of the Dean's stall a lion.   Before both these stalls the ends of the two tiers of desks are richly carved.

The Bishop's throne and Mayor's stall have each a canopied niche on the exterior toward the east,[1] and two small apertures in the east side to enable the occupant to see the altar, and in front of these two stalls the ends of the two tiers of desks are again richly carved. The Mayor's stall, which is wider than the others, was probably that of the Wakeman, and attached to the finial in front is a grotesque ape, beneath which the supporting shaft is of open work. The end of this desk displays a shield charged with two keys in saltire, for the see of York.

The Bishop's throne was originally occupied by the Archbishops of York. The Jacobean canopy, which succeeded that of the fifteenth century, comprised the space of two stalls, as did also the modern structure by which it was itself succeeded and which is now in the Consistory Court. The present canopy resembles those of the other stalls but is higher and more elaborate. Upon the back of the throne inside is a small mitre. The finial in front consists of an elephant carrying a man in his trunk, and bearing on his back a castle filled with armed soldiery, and in front of the elephant is a centaur (renewed), the shaft under which is again of open-work. The end of this desk displays a large mitre above a shield charged with the three stars of St. Wilfrid and supported by two angels, between whom is a scroll with the date 1494.

The Organ occupied the top of the Rood Screen as early as 1408 ; but doubtless all traces of the mediæval instrument disappeared at the Reformation or in the Civil War. During the ascendency of the Puritans organ-building became a lost art, and at the Restoration it had to be revived by foreigners, one of whom, Gerard Schmidt, nephew of ' Father Schmidt,' built an organ for Ripon. This instrument was remodelled in 1833 by Booth of Leeds, and about 1878 the organ was rebuilt by T. C. Lewis of Brixton, so that very little of Schmidt's work now remains. The present case was designed by Sir Gilbert Scott. Over the doorway in the screen is a projecting wooden gallery, in good imitation of the Perpendicular manner. This

[1] It has been supposed that these niches were for figures of St. Peter and St. Wilfrid, and that the same was the case with the two niches which form the ends of the lower tier in the Rood Screen, and also with those which flank the west doors. It may also have been the case with the two eastward projections (if there were two) from the western piers of the Central Tower.

gallery, which dates probably from the time of Schmidt, was occupied until comparatively recently by the organist.   From

Ronald P. Jones, Photo.]

THE WEST END OF THE CHOIR.

the front of it projects a well-carved hand, which, worked by a pedal, could be made to beat time—a very interesting piece of mechanism, which again probably dates from the time of Schmidt.

The North Choir Aisle.—The floor of the choir is now a step above that of the aisles, and it may be further remarked that in both of them the first bay is somewhat dark, being walled up on three sides; that in the second bay the archway toward the choir is occupied by organ-pipes; that a bench table runs along the side wall and the east end, and that the latter portion is adorned with panelling of the same design with the reredos.

Ronald P. Jones, Photo.]

THE NORTH CHOIR AISLE.

In the north aisle the first three bays and a portion of the fourth are Archbishop Roger's work, with the exception of the windows. The most notable feature, as usual, is the vaulting-shafts, which spring from above the string-course, and are in clusters of three. In each cluster the central shaft is even thicker than the others, and the capitals, which are carved with foliage of Norman character, share a common five-sided abacus, while the bases are circular and rest on radiating brackets smaller than themselves. These brackets, which are said to be unique, have square corners and are moulded, but only on the front, and their receding portion consists of a concave moulding containing a convex block. In the north-west corner there is but a single shaft, which rises from the bench-table, is banded at the string-course, and has a square-topped capital. The vaulting has wall-

H

ribs, cross-springers, and groin-ribs, and is rather high-pitched. Upon the cross-springers the mouldings are a large keeled round having on either side a hollow between fillets, while the groin-ribs are moulded as in the Markenfield Chapel. In the westernmost bay the vault has shown signs of weakness (like so many other parts of the building adjacent to

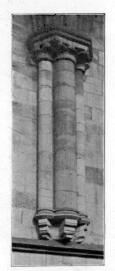

the ill-fated tower) and has been strengthened by a cross-arch with a half-arch abutting against it on the west side, both springing from corbels. The corbels are quite in Archbishop Roger's manner, and indicate that these strengthening arches, and therefore the blocking walls from which they spring, are of his period. Moreover, the abacus moulding of the first choir capital is continued as a string to the shaft (which it encircles) in the north-west corner. This string is interrupted by a rather inexplicable round arch in the west wall, and has also been broken by the obtrusion of the Perpendicular tower-pier, and by the blocked doorway which once opened from the Rood Screen. Below this doorway (adjoining which there is a recess in the obtruding masonry of the tower-pier) the wall shows traces of a gallery or staircase.

Watson, Ripon, Photo.]

TRANSITIONAL VAULTING CORBEL. CHOIR AISLE.

On the north wall the string-course, which is rather undercut, is original as far as the end of the fourth bay, and marks the level to which the sills of the original windows descended in steps.[1] In the present windows, which descend to the old level, the mouldings of the arch are stopped upon a set-off and the jamb is left plain.

In the two easternmost bays the Decorated string-course is of a different pattern and at a slightly higher level ; and here

---

[1] Below the string-course there is a certain amount of limestone in the wall, but this hardly accounts for the language of a Chapter minute which records a meeting in 1546 to consider the repair of certain *defectus et ruinositates apertae tam campanilis quam muri lapidei insulae borealis.*

the jambs of the windows are moulded with a hollow continued from the arch; while the rim of the latter has upon it a large filleted round flanked by hollows and supported on shafts with polygonal plinths and circular bases and capitals, the latter enriched with foliage. The east window, however, is not splayed, and has a deep rear-vault and a flat sill, while its rim is more elaborately moulded and there are shafts to the inner as well as to the outer arch. Except in the two easternmost windows on the north side, the glass is very poor. The Decorated vaulting-shafts are again in clusters of three, but rise from the bench-table and break the string-course. They have polygonal plinths, and their capitals are adorned with rather ill-cut foliage. In the north-east corner there is a single shaft having a fillet, and adjoining it is a round-headed doorway, which once opened into the angle staircase. In this aisle the panelling is carried two bays westwards.

It should be noticed that toward the aisle the choir arches have one more order in the three Decorated bays than they have in the rest. In the Decorated vaulting several chamfers are introduced among the mouldings of the cross-springers, and both in these and in the groin-ribs the most prominent moulding has a fillet. Otherwise the roof roughly matches that of the older bays. The older and the later period meet in the fourth bay from the west, where two of the groin-ribs have the fillet, while the other two are without it. In the two easternmost bays there are fine bosses at the crown of the vault.

It is thought that the Shrine of St. Wilfrid was in the east end of this aisle.[1] Unfortunately Leland's words *S. Wilfridi reliquiae sub arcu prope magnum altare sepultae* are too vague to decide its exact position.

The South Choir Aisle.—This aisle, in some respects, has been altered more than the other, but the south wall is Archbishop Roger's work as far as the end of the fourth bay, if not farther. About 14 feet from the west end occurs that

---

[1] Above the shrine there hung, apparently, a gilded crescent like that above the site of St. Thomas's shrine at Canterbury. The bones were enclosed in a splendid coffer with poles attached, and on solemn occasions this 'feretory,' besides being carried in procession, was sometimes placed under a tent in the fields. It was also very elaborately renewed in 1520 (*Surtee's Soc.*, vol. lxxxi. p. 204, n., etc.). Portions of the shrine exist, perhaps, in the alabaster bas-reliefs in the Chapter-house, as well as in the base of the railing in the north aisle of the nave.

' straight joint ' in the masonry which shows the separation of this aisle from the Mallory Chapel to have been an afterthought ; and a little further east a round-headed doorway, moulded with the edge-roll and retaining a panelled door of some age, opens into the Chapter-house. There was evidently a second and similar doorway a few yards further on, but it has been blocked (doubtless when the cross-wall was built at the back of it between the Chapter-house and vestry), and a square-headed doorway has been made to open into the latter. To the right of this entrance is a square-headed lavatory with a projecting rectangular basin and a hole knocked through into the lobby behind. This lavatory is of course an insertion, probably of the fifteenth century ; indeed the whole of this part of the wall has been much repaired with limestone. The aisle is some-what darkened by the fact that its first four windows look into the Lady-loft. Fortunately the three westernmost are original. They are as usual round-headed and plainly splayed, and their sills descend to the string-course in steps. Archbishop Roger's vaulting-shafts here are in better preservation than in the other aisle. The original vaulting itself must of course have been taken down when the three westernmost columns of the choir-arcade were rebuilt, but in the reconstruction the old ribs seem to have been used again. The groin-ribs have no room to descend upon the Perpendicular choir-capitals, and end pre-maturely upon corbels carved into faces.

The westernmost bay of the aisle has been divided into two storeys, the upper of which now contains part of the mechanism of the organ, but is thought to have been once a chantry chapel. This curious chamber is reached through a pointed doorway at the top of the Library staircase in the south transept. Its roof is of course formed by the aisle-vault, which originally extended, doubtless, as far west-wards in this aisle as in the other. The space, however, has been shortened by the great thickness of a Perpendicular cross-arch, which, though its southern respond obtrudes into the aisle below, is itself only visible from this chamber. When, therefore, the vaulting here was rebuilt, it had to be adapted to the shortened space, and the groin-ribs, which are very much of Archbishop Roger's pattern, spring from Per-pendicular corbels carved into faces. The wall which separates this bay of the aisle from the choir was said above, quite truly, to be Perpendicular, but on this its southern face the masonry is apparently Archbishop Roger's. It is of gritstone, and behind the organ-bellows there remains a corbel like those of the cross-arch that props the vaulting in the corresponding bay of the north aisle. The presumption therefore is that the original vaulting was similarly propped here, and that the wall on which this corbel remains was built to block or strengthen the first choir-arch, and has survived the arch itself. To the west of the door a small square window looks into the Mallory Chapel.

In its eastern portion this aisle resembles the other, but the bench-table here is only carried two bays westward, and the panelling only one bay. In the fifth bay from the west the window is shortened to about half the length of the others, and the string-course (which is of Archbishop Roger's pattern) is correspondingly raised, possibly because a longer window would have come below the springing of the vestry roof (in the period when there was no Lady-loft), or possibly (though this is less likely) to make room for the monument underneath, which, though placed here by Sir Gilbert Scott, who found it in pieces, may have occupied this position before. The monument is that of Moses Fowler, first Dean of Ripon (d. 1608), and the effigy is not a favourable example of English sculpture in the seventeenth century. Of the stained glass, that in the last window on the south side is of some merit. The capitals of the Decorated vaulting-shafts are better executed in this aisle than in the other. Here, as there, the Decorated vaulting begins in the middle of the fourth bay, where the fillet is again found upon the two eastern groins only. At the south-east corner of this aisle are the remains of a piscina—a fragment of a basin resting on a shaft—which probably belonged to one of the many chantries. The staircase at this corner affords the best access to the turret cell described in the last chapter, and to the attic over the choir, where the framing of the roof is a very remarkable specimen of modern joinery.

On account of the alterations that have taken place at different periods in the part of the Cathedral south of the choir, it will be well to examine the crypt under the Chapter-house before examining either the latter itself or the Library.

The Norman Crypt.—A round-headed doorway in the west wall of the Chapter-house admits to a staircase which, roofed with a sloping barrel-vault and descending southwards, turns eastwards, under another round arch, into the crypt. The age of this staircase is uncertain, but its west wall is of course the east wall of Archbishop Roger's transept, and its barrel-vault is under his buttresses which will be seen in the Library. The crypt is divided by a cross-wall with a round arch in it into two portions, each having the vaulting supported on pillars along the middle; but half of the first and third bays of the western portion has been walled up in modern times for burial-

Watson, Ripon, Photo.]

THE NORMAN CRYPT.

vaults. The width of the crypt is about 18 feet and the total length about 68 feet.

This part of the church was assigned by Walbran to Thomas of Bayeux (1070–1100), and by Sir Gilbert Scott to Thurstan (1114–1141); but it is quite possible that both these Archbishops, if not Oda or Oswald before them, may have had a share in its construction. Much of the work at anyrate belongs to a Norman church which preceded that of Archbishop Roger.

In the vaulting (which by-the-way has had to be propped

at some period by two rude pointed limestone arches at the
west end) the chamfered groin-ribs seem to have been added later
for strength, probably when the storey above was remodelled ;
but the vaulting itself, with its square pillars, its plain round
arches from pillar to pillar and from pillar to walls, and
without ribs upon the groins (such having been its original
condition, apparently), seems pure Norman work.[1]   The traces
of painted decoration remaining upon both pillars and vaulting
are probably original.   Along the walls the arches spring, not
from corbels, but from short strings of the same pattern with
the impost-moulding on the pillars—a pattern not of very early
character.   The north and south walls must, perhaps, be as old
at least as the vaulting which rests against them ; nor does the
former wall seem quite on the same plane with the portion of
Archbishop Roger's choir foundations visible outside (between
the present choir and the apse), he having perhaps built his
wall against this one.   The large limestone buttress against this
wall, and another buttress which rises from the east wall but is
hidden by the vaulting, were added in the Decorated period,
and can be followed up through the two storeys above.   They
terminate in the pinnacles of the flying buttresses that span
the choir-aisle.   The south wall may perhaps be definitely
placed somewhat early in the Norman period, since the windows
are splayed both internally and externally.[2]   Of equal
age, probably, is the cross-wall (which, to judge from
the mass of masonry that spans the present passage of com-
munication between the two parts of the crypt, is very thick)
since allowance is made for its thickness in the spacing of the
windows.[3]   It is at least as old as the vaulting, whose bays are
arranged to suit it ; and moreover the half-pillar against its
eastern side has never been a whole pillar, as the capital plainly
shows.   This last remark applies also to the half-pillar against
the extreme west wall, which therefore may perhaps be taken
as marking the westward limit of the crypt at the time when
the vaulting was constructed ; while the east wall (excluding

[1] It may, however, be later than the main walls.
[2] The lower portion of this wall seems to be of an even earlier type of
masonry than the upper.   A somewhat similar difference between the
upper and lower portions may be observed in the east and north walls
also.
[3] The late doorway approached by four steps, east of the cross-wall,
occupies the place of one of the windows.

the apse) probably marks the contemporary eastward limit—if,
that is to say, the eastern portion of the vaulting has not undergone alteration. That eastern portion is clearly planned for an
apse or chancel of some kind. The arch that rises eastward from
the last pillar is stopped half-way in its course by a cross-arch
opening into the apse, and the two last groin-ribs are carried
from the pillar to the abutments of the cross-arch, being obliged
by this contraction of span to form the only pointed arches in
the whole vaulting. Such an arrangement—a 'nave' terminating in an apse, and at the same time divided by a row of
pillars along the middle—is somewhat unusual. The present
apse is of uncertain date. Part of it may be Norman. Its
window indeed is of early Norman type: yet its wall seems of
softer stone than the rest of the crypt,[1] and the string which
runs along the east wall of the latter and round the responds
of the cross-arch is there broken off: moreover, the cross-arch
itself is clearly not of the same date or construction with the
two ribs of the apse-roof, which ribs may possibly be of the
same date as the groin-ribs; and lastly, it will be remembered
that the shafts on the exterior had something of the appearance of Archbishop Roger's work. The floor of the apse is
raised on two steps, but there is no trace of an altar.

It will be noticed that at the south-east corner there is no
apsidal chamber to correspond to that in the storey above.
There is, however, an unsavoury hole from which have been
extracted a number of skulls. Indeed, this crypt formerly
contained huge piles of bones, which had probably been
brought here by the sixteenth century builders from the foundations of their new nave-aisles,[2] and which were removed in
1865 to a pit in the graveyard. Among the stone relics
which have found a resting-place here, the most interesting are
a sarcophagus, the head of a cross of Saxon character, and a
group of coffin-lids near the north wall. Most of these last are
perhaps of the thirteenth century.[3] At the west end of the
crypt is preserved Blore's reredos.

[1] Three kinds of stone occur in this crypt : a sandstone, a fine gritstone,
and a coarser and harder gritstone.

[2] There are numerous entries in the Fabric Rolls, from 1512 onwards,
relating to expenses 'for the carriage of the bones.'

[3] One has a sword graven upon it, another a pair of shears (closed),
another a book and a chalice, the latter slightly tipped, while a gravestone
lying in the apse has upon it a dagger, and a pair of shears open.

The Chapter-house is 22 feet wide from wall to wall and 35 feet long, but it was evidently once open to the vestry, and the dividing wall, which with its bench-table is of limestone, was erected in the Decorated or in the Perpendicular period. In both rooms, as also in the storey above, the original floor was perhaps of stone or tiles, but if so, it has been covered or superseded by wooden planking.

The Chapter-house is marked as such by the stone benches which are carried in two tiers along the north and south walls. On the north side the upper tier is interrupted by the piers of an arcading of plainly chamfered round arches, the central bay of which contains a fine mediæval cupboard with iron scroll-work. The doorway into the choir is very curiously treated on this side. It is surmounted first by a lintel, the stones above which are wedges forming a 'flat arch,' and then by a round arch so high as to run up behind the westernmost arch of the arcading. The very fine vaulting, although some have ascribed it to the Early English period, belongs more probably to the time of Archbishop Roger. Unlike that over the choir-aisles and the Markenfield chapel, however, it has all its arches rounded, and is without wall-ribs. It springs from five-sided corbels which, like the corbels of the old nave, are finished off with scrolls, and which on the north side are placed against the piers of the arcading ; and in the middle of the room it is supported on two cylindrical and monolithic pillars. The bases and capitals of these are circular, and the former are almost pure Early English, the plinth having a round moulding at the bottom, and the base proper consisting of two round mouldings separated by a hollow, with one or two beads or fillets. The capitals are less advanced in style, as the part just above the bell is not moulded and the abacus retains the square edge. All the eight ribs that rise from each pillar resemble the groin-ribs in the crypt.

The arcade against the north wall is continued in the vestry, and it has been thought that it is Norman, and that its arches were once open.[1] But had this ever been the case the piers

[1] Since it is probable that the axis of the church has always, at all periods, passed over the Saxon crypt, the Chapter-house and vestry can hardly have been the south aisle of the choir before the time of Archbishop Roger (as Walbran supposed), for they are too far south ; indeed, they would seem rather to have been a chapel thrown out from such an aisle.

THE CHAPTER-HOUSE.

would surely have been narrower, and would have had capitals. Indeed, it is doubtful whether the arcade is Norman at all : for if it were, its bays might be expected to agree in span and number , with the (presumably Norman) bays of the crypt, whereas there are five bays there and only four here occupying the same total length. Secondly, the set-off on which its piers stand is probably Archbishop Roger's work, as will appear later ; and the piers themselves seem to be of the same construction with the wall behind them, which again is almost certainly his. Moreover, it is significant that the arches agree in span with those of his choir, and that their piers are back to back with his vaulting-shafts in the choir-aisle. Lastly, these piers correspond in width with his buttresses on the north side of the choir. In fact it is difficult to resist the conclusion that they are Archbishop Roger's south choir buttresses in disguise,[1] and that the arches between them were thrown across merely to form a straight boundary for the vaulting, and to carry a ledge which (when there was no storey above) might support the external roof. The piers indeed are carried up, with a 'straight joint' on either side, above the springing of the arches, and the latter are constructed as if they had been let into the piers as an after-thought.[2]

As the bays of this arcade, to which the vaulting is adapted, do not agree with those of the crypt, it follows that the two cylindrical pillars here do not stand exactly over the pillars below—which strengthens the presumption that the vaulting there is of earlier date, and that its groin-ribs were added later for strength : nor does the dividing wall here stand exactly over the cross-wall below, so that the strain on the crypt roof must be considerable.

The two round windows are very widely splayed, and the uppermost part of their rim has a different curvature from the rest, as if they had once been straight-sided and round-headed. In their present form they are of uncertain date. The most conspicuous instance of the employment of this rare type of window—viz., the nave of Southwell Cathedral—is

[1] In the storey above will be found certain buttresses which are clearly his, which stand exactly over these piers, and of which the latter are probably merely the lower portions.

[2] The supposition that the arches were added afterwards would explain why the westernmost of them cuts off the top of the arch over the door.

pure Norman, but the received opinion ascribes these Ripon examples to the time of Archbishop Roger, and it will be observed that their position harmonizes with the bays of the vaulting, which is presumably his, but has no relation externally to the spacing of the windows of the crypt, which, moreover, have an external splay. The third window was once circular like the rest, for a portion of the rim may still be traced; but as it would otherwise have been bisected by the cross-wall, the

Watson, Ripon, Photo.]

The Resurrection.   St. Wilfrid.   The Coronation of the Virgin.

ANCIENT SCULPTURES PRESERVED IN THE CHAPTER-HOUSE.

later builders have blocked half of it and squared the rest, splaying it at the same time like a squint. The date of the south wall itself is doubtful. It is thinner here than in either the vestry or the crypt.

Near the modern hearth is a case of curiosities found about the church, among them several fourteenth or fifteenth century reliefs in alabaster, representing the Resurrection, the Coronation of the Virgin, the story of Herodias, and the figure of a bishop, probably St. Wilfrid, with a curious P-shaped implement on his arm.

At the north end of the cross-wall it will be observed that the blocked doorway noticed in the choir-aisle was not round-headed on this side, but segmental. The square-headed doorway in the cross-wall itself is modern, and opens into a lobby, the opposite side of which is formed by the Decorated buttress whose lower portion was noticed in the crypt, while on the left is the doorway into the choir, and on the right another square-headed doorway, opening into the vestry.

The Vestry.—Before the erection of the cross-wall the vaulting evidently extended eastward continuously to the apse, which still contains a fragment of it with two corbels, while further traces, including another corbel, may be seen upon the south wall. Its removal may have taken place either when the two Decorated buttresses were introduced, or at the erection of the Lady-loft, or possibly much later ; but was doubtless contemporaneous with the building of the cross-wall, which was evidently intended not only as a partition, but as a 'stop' for the portion of the vaulting that was retained. The present ceiling was put up by Sir Gilbert Scott, who, it is said, would have restored the vaulting had funds allowed. Of the buttresses, that adjoining the doorway has in its front, as well as in the side toward the lobby, a small trefoiled and moulded recess. These two buttresses are built against the piers of the arcading, part of the last arch of which is visible behind the cupboard.

In the same cupboard may be observed, scarcely above the floor, a wide stone ledge with a bold moulding worked along the front. If the floor can ever have been lower than it is now, this ledge may have been used as a bench. In itself, it is of course the set-off on which the piers of the arcading stand. Now it will be remembered that the portion of Archbishop Roger's wall-base visible from the graveyard (between the choir and the apse) has at the top a wide set-off or slope. This ledge in the vestry, then, seems to be level with the base of that slope, where moreover there is a moulding similar to that found here ; also the front of the ledge here seems to be flush with Archbishop Roger's masonry there.

If, then, the work there is his,[1] the above considerations afford some reason surely for the belief that this set-off on

[1] That it is his can hardly be doubted. The moulding and slope at the top resemble those which characterize the wall-base throughout his work.

which the piers of the arcading stand, and perhaps also the uppermost courses of the wall beneath it, are Archbishop Roger's work. Nor is it improbable that this set-off once had a slope, of which that above-mentioned was the continuation, and out of which the buttresses (*i.e.*, the arcade piers) rose after the manner of those on the other side of the choir—in fact, that Archbishop Roger intended to make this wall the exterior of his church by demolishing the crypt, vestry, and Chapter-house; and that it was only after some such idea had been conceived and abandoned, that the arches were thrown across from buttress to buttress, the vaulting constructed against them, this ledge formed (by cutting away the slope of the set-off), and the stone benches carried along the wall of the Chapter-house.

The arch above the ledge has been mutilated to make way for a modern spiral staircase of wood leading to the Library. Half-way up this staircase there remain upon the wall and upon the buttress (if it may now be so called) portions of a string-course which may be taken perhaps as additional evidence for the theory that Archbishop Roger at first intended to demolish the vestry and Chapter-house.[1] It does not, however, match the external string on the other side of the choir, but resembles the internal string in the choir-aisles.

The single window in the south wall is round-headed internally, and is partially splayed on one side and not at all on the other: indeed the wall here appears to have undergone some alteration. In this room this wall is of the same thickness with the corresponding wall of the crypt, which is not the case in the Chapter-house.

East of the above window a square-headed doorway opens into the apsidal chamber enclosed by the corner buttress. This curious little chamber was probably a sacristy or treasury. It has a recess in the west side, and seems to have communicated directly with the graveyard. In the roof is a slab which has a small cross graven upon it, and which may have formed part of an altar.

The projection at the south side of the apse was probably one of the responds of an arch against which the vaulting abutted, as in the crypt. Under the east window the curve of the wall has been flattened, probably to afford a better back for the altar, of which the step remains. On the north side is an

---

[1] *Murray's Cathedrals*, Pt. 1, p. 180.

aumbry, with a recess adjoining it in the side of the buttress ; and on the south side is a smaller aumbry, and a piscina with a projecting basin and a semicircular head, the latter cut apparently in one stone. This again is probably one of the earliest piscinæ in existence. The curve of the apse is wider in this storey than below, which partly accounts for the fact that the adjoining Decorated buttress protrudes here into the room. There is also a difference in the stone used, and in several other particulars, *e.g.*, the two windows here have very little external splay—all of which may or may not indicate a difference in date between the apse in this storey and in the crypt. The hand of Archbishop Roger seems traceable here not only in the external shafts and corbel-table, but also in the trefoiling (externally) of the east window. The two vaulting-corbels at any rate seem to be his, as well as the piscina. The upper part of the apse has lost its semicircular shape and been squared, and some masonry has been thrown across from its wall to the Decorated buttress, the motive having been perhaps to make a better support for the rectangular east end of the Lady-loft. The oak table in this room was probably the Communion-table of the church during the period following the Reformation.

The question now arises how long the vestry and Chapterhouse have served their present purpose. Of the arrangements in this storey before the time of Archbishop Roger nothing can be recovered with certainty, but the (presumably Norman) wall between the two parts of the crypt suggests by its thickness that it was intended to support a division of some kind above. After being remodelled in the time of Archbishop Roger, however, this upper storey was evidently open from end to end, and its apsidal termination, containing both piscina and altar-step, indicates that it was a chapel : indeed, as has been well suggested, it was probably the original Lady Chapel. Nevertheless, in an age when every action of life was invested with a religious character, the western part may have been used for capitular purposes even without a dividing wall, and the gritstone benches, so significant of those purposes, are doubtless of considerable age. The statement in the old Records that the trial of 1228 [1] was held *apud Rypon in Aulâ Capituli* is definite enough to show that

[1] See Chapter I.

UNIVERSITY COLLEGE WINCHESTER
LIBRARY

there was a recognised place for Chapter meetings; nor is it
improbable that the reference may be to the present building.
Some doubt is thrown upon this conclusion by a proclamation
of Archbishop Lee in 1537 sequestrating the Common Fund
on the ground that "the Chapter-house is ruinous in walls,
roof, and stonework generally, so that it is likely to fall."
These words, it has been thought, can never have been appli-
cable to the present Chapter-house, and it has been suggested
therefore that there may have been another which has disappeared. Archbishop Lee's words, however, are perhaps not
irreconcilable with the present building. They may refer to
the serious settlement which necessitated the huge Perpendicular buttress at the corner of what is now the vestry. There
is, it is true, some difficulty in the fact that it is not the vestry
but the Chapter-house which is mentioned, and in the
allusion to a dilapidated roof (*tectura*); but it is conceivable
that there was as yet no dividing wall, that the vaulting
of what is now the vestry was still standing, that it had
been injured by the settlement above-mentioned—in fact
that its removal and the erection of the dividing wall took
place in the time of Archbishop Lee. His direction for repairs
may also account for the presence of limestone in the north
wall of the Chapter-house, and for the propping of the vault at
the west end of the crypt.[1] As has already been shown, the
history of the vestry is bound up with that of the Chapter-
house. At what period services ceased to be held at the altar
in the apse, it is difficult to say; perhaps on the completion of
a Lady Chapel above, perhaps on the erection of the dividing
wall,[2] perhaps through the advent of the Reformation. At any
rate, it was probably not before this part of the church had
ceased to be used for services that it began to be recognised
as a robing-room. There is an allusion to a recognised vestry
in Leland, and very possibly the present room is meant; if so,
it would seem from his account to have been used also as a
library. But the fact remains that the church possesses no
vestry except what is obviously a disused chapel.

[1] A view of the crypt as it was before the removal of the bones represents
the vaulting as propped also by certain pillars of Perpendicular character.
These may have been removed by Sir Gilbert Scott.
[2] *I.e.*, if that wall was not erected contemporaneously with the said Lady
Chapel.

The Lady-chapel or Lady-loft is 23 feet 3 inches wide, and 68 feet long.[1] Its west and north sides, being formed by what was once the exterior of the church, display not only windows and buttresses, but also a string-course with gargoyles. From the west wall projects one of Archbishop Roger's buttresses, terminating in a slope, between the two blocked windows of the Mallory Chapel, which resemble the aisle windows of the other transept. The window on the right, mutilated by the insertion of the doorway, has lost its shafts, and retains only their capitals. The other window is partly cut off by the south wall, and is now a cupboard.

In the north wall, the first three bays are Archbishop Roger's, and the windows resemble in their treatment the two just described, and are separated from each other by two buttresses which terminate, like those on the opposite side of the choir, in two slopes one close below the other. There is a third buttress, terminating in a single slope, at the angle formed with the transept. The Decorated window in the fourth bay is treated in the same manner as the rest of those in the eastern portion of the choir-aisles, and the Decorated buttresses which flank it are those which have been followed up from the crypt. The rich string-course or cornice along the top of this and the west wall corresponds with that on the other side of the church. The gargoyles are of course Decorated, and so is the string-course itself, eastwards at any rate of the second gargoyle on the north wall, for here one of the mouldings has a fillet upon it. Whether the rest of the string is Archbishop Roger's work or not, it is difficult to decide.

The large windows in the south and east walls are surmounted by square labels ending in heads. Above the modern fireplace is the defaced monument of Anthony Higgin, second Dean (d. 1624), the founder of the present library; and further east, under the small lancet window (which is filled with fragments of stained glass), is an arched recess of considerable size, and a trefoiled piscina, each surmounted by a gable moulding with a finial. The piscina probably belonged to the chantry of Our-Lady-in-the-Lady-loft. A large stone bracket, supported by a grotesque figure, projects from the east wall, and the east window is bright with armorial bearings of benefactors of the church. This glass, which is mostly of the eighteenth century,

[1] For its date see Chapters I. and II.

I

was once in the great window of the choir. The north side of the recess in which the east window is set, is partially splayed outwards to join the last Decorated buttress, which with its neighbour have been cut back in this storey to the plane of the pinnacles above—doubtless when this Lady-loft was added.

The present pinewood ceiling was put up by Sir Gilbert Scott, but most of the carved angle-pieces in the panels came from an older roof of oak.

Ronald P. Jones, Photo.]

THE LIBRARY.

The history of the library begins with the MS. of the Gospels given by St. Wilfrid; and the ascription to him of various other gifts, which occurs in the writings of Peter of Blois (a Canon of Ripon in the twelfth century), implies at any rate that there was a library when Peter wrote. In 1466 money was bequeathed by William Rodes, a chaplain, *ad fabricam cujusdam librarii in ecclesiâ construendi*, words which may refer to the screening off for books of a portion of this chapel; but in

Leland's time books were apparently kept in the vestry, though it is not certain that the present vestry is meant.[1] Except a few MSS. of Chapter Acts, Fabric Rolls, etc., none of the books now here are known for certain to have belonged to the church before the Reformation;[2] indeed the present collection began with the bequest of his books by Dean Higgin in 1624. The books were in this chapel in 1817, but in 1859 they were at the Deanery. There are now over 5000 volumes, including seven MSS., of which one of the most notable is the Ripon Psalter (1418), containing the special offices for St. Wilfrid, and many printed books of the fifteenth and sixteenth centuries, among them two fine Caxtons. Many of the books have beautiful old bindings in stamped leather. The most interesting items in the collection are exposed in a glass case at the east end of the room.[3] Near the opposite end is another case containing the bones recently dug up under the site of the mediæval altar in the Saxon crypt.

[1] Can Leland mean that the books, then as now, were in the Lady-loft, and that part of it was used as a vestry?

[2] In 1567 a number of books were found in 'a vawte' of the church, where they had been concealed for safety (*Surtees Soc.*, vol. lxxxi. p. 344).

[3] For a full account of this interesting library, see the monograph by the Rev. Canon Fowler, F.S.A., of Durham, by whom the books were arranged in 1872. A copy is kept in the room.

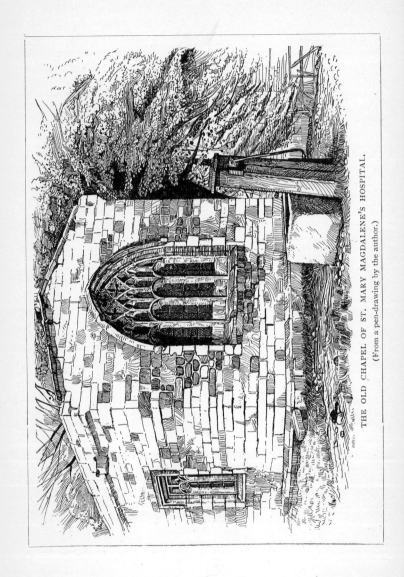

THE OLD CHAPEL OF ST. MARY MAGDALENE'S HOSPITAL.

(From a pen-drawing by the author.)

CHAPTER IV.

OTHER OLD BUILDINGS IN RIPON.

The Deanery, a stone house with two gabled wings, stands opposite to the north transept. It was built in or about 1625. The front bears the royal arms, and the hall contains some paintings of the kings and queens of England, which are more curious than valuable, and are probably of no very great age. Before the house is an ancient stone wall with strongly-marked base, gable coping, and a doorway whose trefoil head was apparently not made for its present position. This may perhaps be part of Abbot Huby's wall, or of the boundary-wall of either the Palace or the Bedern.

Near the south-west tower is a fine red-brick house which doubtless remembers the Georges, or even Queen Anne. It has all the air of a prebendal residence, but if it was ever connected with the church, that connection has long ceased.

Another red-brick house of some age, adjoining the picturesque ascent from High St. Agnesgate to the south transept, was the Canons' Residence up to 1859, when was bought the present Residence near the north-east corner of the graveyard.

High St. Agnesgate contains several interesting buildings, foremost among which is **St. Anne's Hospital,**[1] formerly called 'The Maidens' Due' (Maison de Dieu), with its interesting ruined chapel. This is the only one of the three hospitals which was never affiliated to the Collegiate Church. The date of its origin has been placed shortly before 1438, in which year a chantry was founded in its chapel. The hospital foundation was for four poor men and four poor women, and there were also two beds for 'casuals'; and the little community was under the charge of a priest. There was apparently no endowment. The domestic portion of the building was pulled down in 1869. Though it had been divided into cottages some time before that date, the original arrangements have been recovered from an old document and from certain indications that had

---

[1] In the mediæval records the street is almost invariably called Annesgate, and indeed was probably named after the hospital. The form 'Agnesgate' is, however, not modern, for it occurs in 1462. It may have arisen from a trisyllabic pronunciation of 'Annesgate.'

survived in the fabric itself. Joined to the west end of the
chapel was a sort of nave, divided down the middle by a
partition, on one side of which were the beds for the men, on
the other those for the women, while at the west end were
two rooms for the priest. This 'nave' was probably open to
the chapel, as the large size of the western arch of the latter
seems to indicate, and possibly the infirmer inmates could attend
the service without leaving their beds.[1]

To pass to the chapel itself—a window in the north wall has
been blocked with masonry, upon which is a shield of arms,
thought to be those of Sir Solomon Swale of South Stainley,
and surmounted by a Maltese cross with the letters S.S. and
the date 1654 upon it. The west gable has once been
crowned by a bell-cote, and attached to the south-west corner
of the chapel are the remains of an arched doorway. The
western arch of the building, curiously enough, is not in the
middle of the wall. It is recessed and chamfered, and rests
upon two semi-cylindrical responds, whose rather curious
capitals do not follow the form of the shaft, but are triple
and rectangular. The chapel internally is 20 feet 10 inches
long and 11 feet 6 inches wide, and is not at right angles to
its western wall, but inclines considerably toward the south.
In the middle of the entrance is an octagonal basin, supported
on a pedestal and having a shield on each of its sides.
This is thought to have been a stoup for holy water. It is
not, perhaps, in its original position, and the pedestal does
not seem to belong to it. Opposite to the blocked window
already mentioned, which has an aumbry east of it, there is a
late square-headed window of two lights, whose arches do not
reach quite up to the lintel, but are connected with it by
short perpendiculars. East of this is a piscina with projecting semi-octagonal basin, trefoil head, and ogee hood,
and with a small square window above and to the left of it.
The stone slab on two stone supports against the east wall is
probably the original altar, and tradition says that the ransom
of a Scottish prince was paid down upon it. On either side
of the altar is a stone bracket, that on the north side bearing
a shield of arms.[2] The east window, which is blocked, is

[1] Thus far I am largely indebted to a paper on this hospital by the Rev.
W. C. Lukis, F.S.A. in the twelfth edition of Walbran's *Ripon*.
[2] Possibly those of Boynton or Plumpton (*Parker*).

THE CHAPEL OF ST. ANNE'S HOSPITAL.

(From a pen-drawing by the author.)

divided into two lights, and the head is almost filled by a large quatrefoil, of which the uppermost and lowermost foils are ogees. This window, and the piers and capitals of the western arch, give the impression that the chapel is of a date earlier than that usually assigned for the foundation of the hospital. The modern cottages are inhabited by eight women.

Between St. Anne's Hospital and Bondgate Green Bridge stands the **Thorp Prebendal House**, now divided into several dwellings. Whether its existing fabric is as old as the Reformation or not, this was the site upon which dwelt the Canons of the mediæval prebend of Thorp. In 1391 the hall of the then existing house was used for casting several bells for the Minster, and here, in later days, as Canon of Thorp, lived Marmaduke Bradley. The house is said to have been sold by Edward VI. to the Earl of Cumberland, and to have subsequently sheltered Mary Queen of Scots, James I., and Charles I. It is best seen from the adjoining bridge, whence its plastered walls, irregular gables, and stone roof form a picturesque foreground to the Cathedral. Of the dwellings into which it is now divided, the third from the bridge contains the grand staircase, which has twisted skeleton balusters.

East of St. Anne's Hospital, there are two more old houses, one of which, known as **St. Agnes' Lodge**,[1] is of considerable interest. The body of it, long and low, with a high-pitched roof and with a massive chimney-stack buttressing one end, is said to be of the time of Henry VII., but derives much of its 'character' from the comparatively modern windows, which resemble the portholes of a ship. A wing added in the seventeenth century, with quaint curvilinear gable, projects into the garden behind. Within the house is a square hall, having above the fireplace some carving and a painted panel of the burning of London in 1666. There is also a good oak staircase, and in the upper storey are several quaint features, including a cupboard that may have served for a hiding-place, and two 'powdering-closets' in which ladies' hair, or men's wigs, could be powdered in the eighteenth century. But the part of the house most interesting architecturally is the attics, where the framing of the king-post roof is extremely massive, while the floor is of *concrete*.[2] One of the roof-beams in the wing bears the date 1693. This house disputes with the Thorp

[1] The house is not shown.
[2] This latter peculiarity is found also in a house at Bishopton, a mile off.

Prebendal House the honour of having sheltered Mary Queen of Scots on her way from Bolton Castle to Tutbury, and it is said that it was during her sojourn at Ripon that she addressed an appeal to Queen Elizabeth and received an offer of marriage from the Duke of Norfolk. St. Agnes' Lodge claims also to have been a temporary home of Turner, at the time when he was illustrating Whitaker's *History of Craven* and *History of Richmondshire.* Whether this house or its immediately western neighbour were ever prebendal residences it is now difficult to say.

Two old gabled houses remain in the Market-place, and one of them, now a basket-shop, is said to have been the residence of Hugh Ripley, last Wakeman and first Mayor of Ripon.

At the north end of Stonebridgegate, and not far from the Ure, stands the **Hospital of St. Mary Magdalene**, sometimes called 'The Maudlins.' It was founded by Archbishop Thurstan (1114–1141) for secular brethren and sisters, and one chaplain. The brethren and sisters were not merely to benefit by the charity themselves, but were to minister to lepers and blind priests born within the Liberty of Ripon, a certain number of whom were received into the Hospital. Lepers from outside the Liberty were entitled to a night's lodging : so also apparently were any other strangers or mendicant clergy who might be passing through the town. On St. Mary Magdalene's day there was a dole of food to the poor. A second chaplain was subsequently added by the benefaction of one William de Homelyn. At some period, apparently after 1241, the character of the foundation was changed by another Archbishop, whose name is not known. The brethren and sisters disappeared, and the staff consisted henceforth of a Master and one chaplain, or sometimes two. The Master was appointed by the Archbishop, and was generally a clerk, though sometimes only in acolyte's Orders In 1334 one John Warrener, of Studley Roger, founded here a chantry of two if not three priests. Thus there may have been no less than six clergy attached to this small chapel ; but the number was not kept up, and at the Reformation there were, besides the Master, only the two priests of Warrener's foundation. The Hospital continued to minister to blind priests, and also to lepers until leprosy died out. The lepers' portion of the building was demolished about 1350.

In 1546–7 the inmates were 'five poor people.' All traces of the Master's house, the hall, the brewery, and the original dwellings have vanished. The dwellings were rebuilt in 1674, and again in 1875, since which date more cottages have been added, and a new chapel; and the hospital now accommodates twelve poor women. The Mastership, still in the gift of the Archbishop, is at present held with one of the canonries, and the cure of souls is discharged by a non-resident chaplain.

SEAL OF ST. MARY
MAGDALENE'S HOSPITAL.

Fortunately the old chapel remains. The main fabric is apparently Thurstan's. It is of gritstone, but has been much altered and repaired at later periods, when limestone has been used. To the later work belong the set-off of the base, the coigns, the parapet, the east part of the south wall, the framing of most of the windows and doors, and the buttress and bell-cote at the west end.

The west front is now divided by a large buttress of many stages terminating in a slope, but the plinth of this buttress is apparently original. To the right of the buttress is a long two-cusped lancet light; to the left may be traced, perhaps, the outline of an original round-arched window; while on both sides there are sloping lines in the masonry, as if there had been an acutely-pointed gable here.

The north side of the chapel has been propped at a late period by three sloping buttresses. At its western end is a doorway, the jambs of which seem original, while the pointed head is later. About half-way along this side is one of those 'low side windows' through which, it is supposed, the Sacrament was administered to lepers—indeed, the leper-house stood on this side of the chapel.[1] Though of limestone, this small lancet window, with its arch and dripstone trefoiled, is

[1] Some archæologists, however, hold that the purpose of low side windows was to display a light to scare away demons.

apparently of the thirteenth century, and an early example of its class. East of it are, first a Perpendicular window of two lights—late in character, and second a partially-blocked and possibly original doorway, perhaps for the priest, (though priests' doors are usually on the south side). Its outer arch is rounded, while the inner is pointed and has perhaps been altered.

The east window is broad, finely arched, and surmounted by a bold dripstone terminating in heads. Its four lights, partially blocked, are round-headed, with rather large cusps, and in the upper part of the window there is much tracery, in which perpendicular lines lead up to arches that intersect. Indeed it is difficult to say whether this fine window is an example of late Perpendicular, or of the transition to that style from the Decorated.

It is on the south side that the irregularity in the size, spacing, and level of the windows in this chapel is most marked. Here toward the eastern end is a square-headed Perpendicular window of two lights, much resembling the south window at St. Anne's Hospital, and surmounted by a square label. Next comes a small lancet, probably Early English, with no limestone about it. The next window is tall, rectangular, and without tracery, but the stump of a mullion remains on the sill, which is of gritstone. West of this is the principal entrance, a Norman arch, beneath which a pointed arch has been inserted, the original imposts, however, remaining. The upper arch is enriched with the chevron, and its dripstone with two rows of the round billet arranged chequerwise and with a moulding composed of a series of little crosses, rather suggestive of the dog-tooth.

The interior has up to this time escaped 'restoration.' There have been repairs, but enough only to arrest decay, and the plaster has not been removed from the walls.[1] The length internally is about 49 feet and the breadth just over 16 feet. The floor is of brick, and the roof, which is almost flat, has been much renovated, but retains its original massive cross beams and wooden corbels. Internally the two

---

[1] It is probable that in the interior of many of our old churches the surface of the stone was never meant to be seen, and was covered with plaster at the time of building. The plaster was doubtless often adorned with designs in colour.

western doorways are rounded, and just east of them the chapel is crossed by a late Perpendicular screen, which retains its folding doors, and has an uncommon effect due to the great length of the mullions in the upper part. The lower portion was once closed. It is perhaps more probable that this is the original position of the screen than that it ever stretched across the Sanctuary. Against the north wall is a fine old chest raised on feet and bound with many iron clamps ending in scrolls. It has a double lock and a ring at either end, and inside it is kept a curious bell of wood painted to resemble metal, and said to have been hung in the bell-cote by an unscrupulous official who had caused the real bell to be sold.

The 'low side window' internally has a depressed pointed arch, and is widely splayed, as are also the tall and the short window opposite. It is remarkable that although the windows differ so much externally, yet internally all except the 'low side window' and the east window are of the form known as the 'shouldered arch,' a form which, by-the-way, is more usually employed in doorways.

In front of the Sanctuary are preserved two old Perpendicular pews or stalls, with carved finials. The Sanctuary itself is raised on two steps, and extends eight feet from the east wall. The blocked door noticed on the exterior would open into the chapel immediately west of the line of the lower step.

This is among the very few churches in the country which retain the pre-Reformation stone altar, and if the instance at St. Anne's Hospital is genuine, Ripon thus possesses two examples of this rare feature. The altar here is 7 feet 7 inches long, 3 feet 5 inches wide, 2 feet 11 inches high, and has no step. Two of the usual five incised crosses (the larger cross near the middle is probably spurious) may still be traced upon the slab, the lower edge of which is chamfered off. In the front of the substructure are two deep recesses. The altar is flanked by two stone brackets. On the north wall is a third, and in the south wall a piscina with two-cusped arch and projecting basin.

In front of the altar is a tessellated pavement 11 feet long and nearly 4 feet wide. It is chiefly composed of red and blackish *tesseræ*; but in the centre is a circular medallion containing a large four-petalled white flower with a red centre and small red flowers between the petals, all upon a ground of black. It has been supposed that this pavement was taken from the neighbouring remains of some Roman building. As regards the central medallion this is probably the case, but the rest of the pavement seems to be later work, perhaps of the thirteenth century.[1] At the south end of the pavement is the slab of another and smaller altar, retaining three of its incised crosses.

It appears from a document of 1306 that the chapel at that date contained certain 'relics' of St. Mary Magdalene.

Of the mediæval bridges of Ripon **The North Bridge** alone survives.[2] It crosses the Ure on nine arches with bold buttresses, triangular in plan, between them, and is prolonged, with three smaller arches, over the low meadow which forms the southern shore. It is from this shore that the best view of it is to be obtained, a few yards down stream. The arches, some of them recessed, vary in height and span, but all are round save two, over one of which there is a corbel-table below the parapet. The other side of the bridge was remodelled some twenty years ago.

[1] This view is held by Mr. Micklethwaite. The white *tesseræ* in the medallion resemble some which were dug up in 1837 on the site assigned by Leland to the 'Old Abbay of Ripon' and which have been adduced to support the view that Wilfrid's Abbey Church stood on that site and not on the site of the present Cathedral (see p. 77 and n. 4 there).

[2] The others were Bondgate Bridge (over the Skell), Bishopton Bridge (over the Laver), Hewick Bridge (over the Ure below the town), the Archer-bridge, and the 'Esgel-bridge.' The position of the two last is uncertain, and the rest have long been rebuilt. Bishopton Bridge had a chapel upon it with which was connected a hermit. In the middle ages the bridges were under the charge of the Archbishop. They were often the recipients of bequests, but were themselves made to contribute to the Common Fund of the Collegiate Church, by means of money-boxes which were placed upon them.

APPENDIX.

ABBOTS OF THE SAXON MONASTERY.

St. Eata	.	.	.	.	.	c. 657–661.
St. Wilfrid	.	.	.	.	.	661–709.
Tatberht	.	.	.	.	.	709.
Botwine	.	.	.	.	.	709.
Alberht	.	.	.	.	.	died 786.
Sigred	.	.	.	.	.	786–787.
Uilden or Wildeng	.	.	.	.	.	787. ?

CANONS OF STANWICK IN THE MEDIÆVAL COLLEGIATE CHURCH.[1]

Geoffrey de Bockland	.	.	.	.	circa 1226.
Laurence de Topcliffe	.	.	.	.	circa 1230.
Eadmund de Maundevill	.	.	.	.	resigned 1279.
Anthony Beck [2]	.	.	.	.	1279.
Roger Swayne	.	.	.	.	1279.
Richard de Henney	.	.	.	c. 1285–c. 1311.
William de Seton	.	.	.	.	1311–c. 1315.
Thomas de Cave	.	.	.	.	1316–c. 1320.
Robert de Rypon	.	.	.	.	1320–c. 1322.
Peter de Wetwang	.	.	.	.	1322–c. 1333.
John de Crakhall	.	.	.	.	1333.
John de Seggefield	.	.	.	c. 1344–c. 1378.
John de Middleton	.	.	.	.	1378–1384.
John de Dene [3]	.	.	.	.	1384–1397.
Simon Alcock	.	.	.	.	1397–c. 1435.
Richard Morton	.	.	.	.	1435–c. 1436.
John Clere	.	.	.	.	1436–? 1447.
Robert Symson	.	.	.	.	? 1447–1478.
Thomas Bakehouse	.	.	.	.	1479–1481.
Richard Dean	.	.	.	.	1481–c. 1521.
Christopher Seale	.	.	.	.	c. 1535–c. 1545.
					c. 1545–? 1547.

[1] The mediæval College of Canons had no official head, but the Prebendary of Stanwick, as Ruler of the Choir, was generally in residence, and was in some sense the most important of the Canons. He did not, however, preside, at least not if any other Canon was in residence. Thus Christopher Dragley (Prebendary of Monkton) was often *Praesidens Capituli* from 1533 to 1539, and Marmaduke Bradley (Prebendary of Thorp) from 1544 to 1546.

[2] Afterwards the celebrated Bishop of Durham, one of the most prominent personages at the court of Edward I.

[3] A brass to him is preserved in the Cathedral. The inscription was probably cut in his lifetime, for the space for the date of his death is left blank. He helped to found the chantry of St. Wilfrid, and is buried in the Choir.

DEANS OF KING JAMES I.'S FOUNDATION.

Moses Fowler, B.D.	1604–1608.
Anthony Higgin, B.D.	1608–1624.
John Wilson, D.D.	1624–1634.
Thomas Dod, D.D.[1]	1635–c. 1645.
John Wilkins, D.D., F.R.S.[2]	1660–1668.
John Neile, D.D.[3]	1674–1675.
Thomas Tullie, D.D.	1675.
Thomas Cartwright, D.D.[4]	1675–1686.
Christopher Wyvill, D.D.[5]	1686–1710.
Heneage Dering, LL.D.[6]	1710–1750.
Francis Wanley, D.D.[7]	1750–1791.
Robert Darley Waddilove, LL.D., F.S.A.[8]	1792–1828.
James Webber, D.D.	1828–

DEANS OF THE CATHEDRAL FOUNDATION.

James Webber, D.D.[9]	–1847.
The Hon. Henry David Erskine, D.D.[10]	1847–1859.
Thomas Garnier, B.C.L.	1859–1860.
William Goode, D.D., F.S.A.	1860–1868.
Hugh M'Neile, D.D.	1868–1876.
Sydney Turner, B.A.	1876.
William Robert Fremantle, D.D.	1876–1895.
The Hon. William Henry Fremantle, D.D.	1895.

BISHOPS OF RIPON.

EADHEAD	681–686.
CHARLES THOMAS LONGLEY, D.D., F.S.A.[11]	1836–1856.
ROBERT BICKERSTETH, D.D., F.R.S.[12]	1857–1884.
WILLIAM BOYD-CARPENTER, D.D.	1884.

1 Deprived by the Parliament when they suppressed the Chapter.
2 One of the founders of the Royal Society: married Oliver Cromwell's sister: became Bishop of Chester.
3 Buried near the vestry door.
4 Became Bishop of Chester, and was a strong supporter of James II.
5 Buried within the Altar-rails (brass).
6 Buried in the north choir-aisle (tablet).
7 Buried in the Cathedral (formerly there was a tablet in the south aisle of the nave).
8 Tablet in the Chapter-house.
9 Buried within the Altar-rails.
10 Buried in the graveyard near the north-east corner of the choir (tomb by Sir Gilbert Scott).
11 Afterwards Bishop of Durham, then Archbishop of York, and finally Archbishop of Canterbury. The modern diocese of Ripon does not correspond in area with that over which Eadhead presided (see Chap. I.).
12 Buried in the graveyard near the south-east corner of the choir.

INDEX.

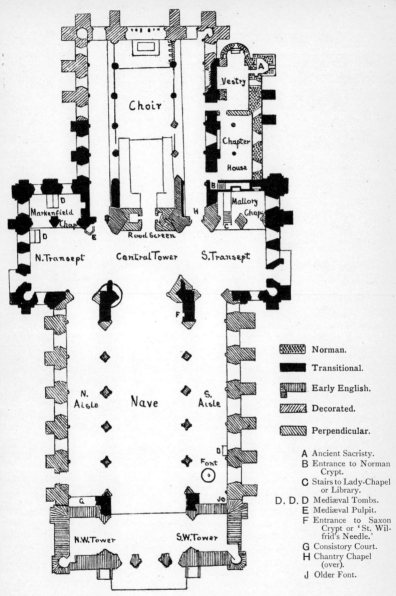

Norman.

Transitional.

Early English.

Decorated.

Perpendicular.

A Ancient Sacristy.
B Entrance to Norman Crypt.
C Stairs to Lady-Chapel or Library.
D, D, D Mediæval Tombs.
E Mediæval Pulpit.
F Entrance to Saxon Crypt or 'St. Wilfrid's Needle.'
G Consistory Court.
H Chantry Chapel (over).
J Older Font.

GROUND PLAN OF RIPON CATHEDRAL.

DIMENSIONS (internal).

Total Length, ...	270 feet
Length of Nave, . . .	133 ,,
Width of Nave, ...	87 ,,
Width of Transept, . . .	52 ,,
Height of Vault (Nave), . .	88 ,,
Height of Towers, . . .	110 ,,
Area, ...	25,280 square feet.

PRINTED BY NEILL AND CO., LTD., EDINBURGH.

Bell's Cathedral Series.

Profusely Illustrated.   Cloth, crown 8vo, 1s. 6d. *net each.*

NOW READY.

ENGLISH CATHEDRALS. An Itinerary and Description. Compiled by JAMES G. GILCHRIST, A.M., M.D. Revised and edited with an Introduction on Cathedral Architecture by the Rev. T. PERKINS, M.A., F.R.A.S.

BRISTOL. By H. J. L. J. MASSÉ, M.A.
CANTERBURY. By HARTLEY WITHERS   3rd Edition, revised.
CARLISLE. By C. K. ELEY.
CHESTER. By CHARLES HIATT. 2nd Edition, revised.
DURHAM. By J. E. BYGATE, A.R.C.A. 2nd Edition.
ELY. By Rev. W. D. SWEETING, M.A.
EXETER. By PERCY ADDLESHAW, B.A. 2nd Edition.
GLOUCESTER. By H. J. L. J. MASSÉ, M.A. 2nd Edition.
HEREFORD. By A. HUGH FISHER, A.R.E. 2nd Edition, revised.
LICHFIELD. By A. B. CLIFTON. 2nd Edition, revised.
LINCOLN. By A. F. KENDRICK, B.A. 2nd Edition, revised.
NORWICH. By C. H. B. QUENNELL. 2nd Edition.
OXFORD. By Rev. PERCY DEARMER, M.A. 2nd Edition, revised.
PETERBOROUGH. By Rev. W. D. SWEETING, M.A. 2nd Edition.
RIPON. By CECIL HALLET, B.A.
ROCHESTER. By G. H. PALMER, B.A. 2nd Edition.
ST. DAVID'S. By PHILIP ROBSON, A.R.I.B.A.
ST. PAUL'S. By Rev. ARTHUR DIMOCK, M.A. 2nd Edition.
SALISBURY. By GLEESON WHITE. 2nd Edition, revised.
SOUTHWELL. By Rev. ARTHUR DIMOCK, M.A. 2nd Edition, revised.
WELLS. By Rev. PERCY DEARMER, M.A. 2nd Edition, revised.
WINCHESTER. By P. W. SERGEANT. 2nd Edition, revised.
WORCESTER. By EDWARD F. STRANGE.
YORK. By A. CLUTTON BROCK. 2nd Edition, revised.

Preparing.

CHICHESTER. By H. C. CORLETTE, A.R.I.B.A.
ST. ALBANS. By Rev. W. D. SWEETING, M.A.
ST. ASAPH'S and BANGOR. By P. B. IRONSIDE BAX.
GLASGOW. By P. MACGREGOR CHALMERS, I.A., F.S.A. (Scot).
LLANDAFF. By HERBERT PRIOR.

Uniform with above Series. 1s. 6d. *net each.*

ST. MARTIN'S CHURCH, CANTERBURY. By Rev. CANON ROUTLEDGE, M.A., F.S.A. 24 Illustrations.
BEVERLEY MINSTER. By CHARLES HIATT. 47 Illustrations.
WIMBORNE MINSTER AND CHRISTCHURCH PRIORY. By Rev. T. PERKINS, M.A., F.R.A.S. 65 Illustrations.
TEWKESBURY ABBEY AND DEERHURST PRIORY. By H. J. L. J. MASSÉ, M.A. 44 Illustrations.
BATH ABBEY, MALMESBURY ABBEY, AND BRADFORD-ON-AVON CHURCH. By Rev. T. PERKINS, M.A.
WESTMINSTER ABBEY. By CHARLES HIATT.   [*Preparing.*

Bell's Handbooks to Continental Churches.

Profusely Illustrated.   Crown 8vo, cloth, 2s. 6d. *net each.*

CHARTRES: The Cathedral and Other Churches. By H. J. L. J. MASSÉ, M.A.   [*Ready.*
ROUEN: The Cathedral and Other Churches. By the Rev. T. PERKINS, M.A.   [*Ready.*
PARIS (NOTRE-DAME). By CHARLES HIATT.   [*Preparing.*

LONDON: GEORGE BELL AND SONS

5.01—R.P.—10,000.

Opinions of the Press.

"For the purpose at which they aim they are admirably done, and there are few visitants to any of our noble shrines who will not enjoy their visit the better for being furnished with one of these delightful books, which can be slipped into the pocket and carried with ease, and is yet distinct and legible. . . . A volume such as that on Canterbury is exactly what we want, and on our next visit we hope to have it with us. It is thoroughly helpful, and the views of the fair city and its noble cathedral are beautiful. Both volumes, moreover, will serve more than a temporary purpose, and are trustworthy as well as delightful."—*Notes and Queries*.

"We have so frequently in these columns urged the want of cheap, well-illustrated, and well-written handbooks to our cathedrals, to take the place of the out-of-date publications of local booksellers, that we are glad to hear that they have been taken in hand by Messrs George Bell & Sons."—*St. James's Gazette*.

"The volumes are handy in size, moderate in price, well illustrated, and written in a scholarly spirit. The history of cathedral and city is intelligently set forth and accompanied by a descriptive survey of the building in all its detail. The illustrations are copious and well selected, and the series bids fair to become an indispensable companion to the cathedral tourist in England."—*Times*.

"They are nicely produced in good type, on good paper, and contain numerous illustrations, are well written, and very cheap. We should imagine architects and students of architecture will be sure to buy the series as they appear, for they contain in brief much valuable information."—*British Architect*.

"Bell's 'Cathedral Series,' so admirably edited, is more than a description of the various English cathedrals. It will be a valuable historical record, and a work of much service also to the architect. The illustrations are well selected, and in many cases not mere bald architectural drawings but reproductions of exquisite stone fancies, touched in their treatment by fancy and guided by art."—*Star*.

"Each of them contains exactly that amount of information which the intelligent visitor, who is not a specialist, will wish to have. The disposition of the various parts is judiciously proportioned, and the style is very readable. The illustrations supply a further important feature; they are both numerous and good. A series which cannot fail to be welcomed by all who are interested in the ecclesiastical buildings of England."—*Glasgow Herald*.

"Those who, either for purposes of professional study or for a cultured recreation, find it expedient to 'do' the English cathedrals will welcome the beginning of Bell's 'Cathedral Series.' This set of books is an attempt to consult, more closely, and in greater detail than the usual guide-books do, the needs of visitors to the cathedral towns. The series cannot but prove markedly successful. In each book a business-like description is given of the fabric of the church to which the volume relates, and an interesting history of the relative diocese. The books are plentifully illustrated, and are thus made attractive as well as instructive. They cannot but prove welcome to all classes of readers interested either in English Church history or in ecclesiastical architecture."—*Scotsman*.

"They have nothing in common with the almost invariably wretched local guides save portability, and their only competitors in the quality and quantity of their contents are very expensive and mostly rare works, each of a size that suggests a packing-case rather than a coat-pocket. The 'Cathedral Series' are important compilations concerning history, architecture, and biography, and quite popular enough for such as take any sincere interest in their subjects."—*Sketch*.

LONDON: GEORGE BELL AND SONS